TO BE
CONTINUED...xx
CLUDED...xx

* HOW TO PREVENT
YOUR PAST FROM
PILING UP AND
FIND HOPE FOR
YOUR FUTURE

TO BE
CONTINUED...xx

MIKE ASHCRAFT

WITH T.L. HEYER

B&H
PUBLISHING
NASHVILLE, TENNESSEE

Published by B&H Publishing Group
Nashville, Tennessee

Dewey Decimal Classification: 153.8
Subject Heading: TIME MANAGEMENT / WORK ETHIC /
ACHIEVEMENT MOTIVATION

Unless otherwise marked, all Scripture quotations
are taken from New International Version®, NIV®
Copyright ©1973, 1978, 1984, 2011 by Biblica, Inc.® Used by
permission. All rights reserved worldwide.

Scripture quotations marked ESV are taken from the English
Standard Version. ESV® Text Edition: 2016. Copyright © 2001 by
Crossway Bibles, a publishing ministry of Good News Publishers.

Scripture quotations marked NASB are taken from the New
American Standard Bible®, copyright © 1960, 1971, 1977, 1995,
2020 by The Lockman Foundation. All rights reserved.

Scripture quotations marked NLT are taken from the New Living
Translation, copyright © 1996, 2004, 2015 by Tyndale House
Foundation. Used by permission of Tyndale House Publishers,
Inc., Carol Stream, Illinois 60188. All rights reserved.

Scripture quotations marked NLV are taken from the New Living
Version, copyright © 1969, 2003 by Barbour Publishing, Inc.

Scripture quotations marked NKJV are taken from
the New King James Version®. Copyright © 1982 by Thomas
Nelson. Used by permission. All rights reserved.

The author is represented by the literary agency of
WordServe Literary, www.wordserveliterary.com.

Cover design by Derek Thornton, Notch Design. Author photo
by Josh Driggs, courtesy of Port City Community Church.

1 2 3 4 5 6 • 26 25 24 23 22

To my parents, Eddie and Margaret Ashcraft: I
have inherited an incredible foundation upon
which to build and learn of God's faithfulness.

To my in-laws, Owings and Brenda Austin: I have
witnessed firsthand the beauty of steadfast faith. The
final chapter of this book is about a beautiful faith and
my tribute to Mr. Austin (1937–2019). We miss you!

ACKNOWLEDGMENTS

I'VE HEARD IT said that some books write themselves . . . this one DID NOT.

It was extracted word by word like teeth! The process has been incredibly rich and I am incredibly thankful . . . here are a few people who I am indebted to and a few reasons why.

Julie (my wife), Michaela (my daughter), Maddie (my daughter), and Carson (my son-in-law): You are my people. Thank you for cheering and celebrating and sacrificing and listening through the process of wrestling and writing.

Tricia: I am thankful that you took the risk to put the ideas and doodles into a readable format so we can invite others into this journey.

Laurelyn: Thank you for connecting me with Tricia and then making countless connections to help this book come together.

Taylor and the team at Lifeway: Thank you for reading this over and over and for believing the message to help others find hope through it.

Thank you to my small group and my friends from PC3 Overflow (our college ministry) for the title testing and the cover design focus groups. Thank you Brian (my brother) who claims he came up with the title, but those claims remain in dispute.

I am profoundly grateful for Port City Church. It is the place where I am privileged to serve as Pastor, but more importantly the place where I've been allowed to grow and explore God's promise of redemption in the real life context of our beautiful community.

CONTENTS

THE NETFLIX LIFESTYLE

To Be Continued . . .

I REMEMBER THE first time I binge-watched a television series on Netflix. I didn't intend to. . . . It just happened.

You might be surprised to learn that my first binge was only about two years ago. I was late to the Netflix game, but it didn't take long for me to see the appeal.

Everybody everywhere seemed to be talking about *Parenthood*, a family-tree drama series about the Bravermans. My wife Julie and I logged on and settled in on the couch. We scrolled through the menu, found the show, and hit play: Season 1, Episode 1. The run time was forty-seven minutes, which felt perfect. I'm not much of a TV-watching guy anymore, but I could commit to forty-seven minutes with no commercials. Let's go.

Sure enough, the Braverman family swept me right into the layered dynamics of their story. They made me laugh;

they made me think—I could see what everyone was talking about.

And then something happened that changed the way I viewed television.

When that first episode ended, a small window popped up at the bottom of the screen, offering a teaser paragraph about the next episode. This was not the life-changing part; I am used to that. Those episode previews existed in my 1980s favorites, *Chips*, *The A-Team*, *Family Ties*, and *Saved by the Bell*.

But do you know what was *not* normal? That little countdown clock.

"Your series will continue in 10 . . . 9 . . . 8 . . . 7 . . ."

Wait, what?!

No time to get up off the couch, no time to get an evening snack of cookies and milk, and certainly no time to go to the bathroom. My series was about to continue. All I had to do was sit there and let one episode roll into the next.

Two seasons later and a whole weekend lost, I realized I had left the couch only because I really had to go to the bathroom. I probably couldn't have told you what each episode was about, since they all blurred into a delicious blend of layered drama. My bloodshot eyes, my racing mind, and my depleted vocabulary would probably have vaguely described the experience as "good."

Parenthood was better than good. Each episode was excellent. But they muddled together in my mind as one long experience rather than a dozen colorful stories with a beginning, middle, and end.

Binge-watching has entered our lives on a number of levels—this habit of consuming as much as we can, as fast as we can, rather than watching the show on the balanced, intentional cadence of regular weekly programming. The term *binge-watching* was even added to the Oxford online dictionary in 2014.[1] It's a word we seem to need for a thing we seem to need to do.

(Listen, I'm not blaming anybody. . . . If binge-watching had been an option in the eighties, I promise you I'd have lost hundreds of consecutive hours hanging out with *The A-Team*.)

Often we live our lives like a binge-watch, in a perpetual mode of "to be continued." This pattern may be great for Netflix, but a chronic continuation is no way to live. We have lost the rhythms of sabbath and sunrise, of mealtime and bedtime. These ideas have been replaced by phrases like "burn the midnight oil" and "the early bird gets the worm," and they have planted seeds of perpetual anxiety. The pace keeps accelerating, and there is no built-in commercial break for snacks, no margin to process what just happened.

This is how the past gets dragged into the future: when one episode continues into the next, we don't even notice that the season ended. Without finish lines, we become bystanders in our own lives, without a clear understanding of how to truly live.

Continuation is what happens when there is no conclusion.

We don't need continuations. We need conclusions.

Many seasons have clearly defined conclusions, like New Year's Eve or high school graduation. There are times when everyone knows when it's over.

But other endings are vague—like the transition from mullets (are these *really* back?) and flattop haircuts, the finish line from winter to spring, or the long journey to healing from grief, disappointment, and loss.

Sometimes the conclusion is so subtle we don't notice it, and sometimes we discover the conclusion far too late, when we're left holding only regret or hindsight.

> CONTINUATION IS WHAT HAPPENS WHEN THERE IS NO CONCLUSION. WE DON'T NEED CONTINUATIONS. WE NEED CONCLUSIONS.

Sometimes we have to move into the next thing without knowing what is next.

Uncertainty can hold us captive and make us second-guess everything, or it can be a catalyst for a process.

Conclusions aren't just about the outcome; they're about the process.

Sometimes the point of the journey is the journey.

The word *conclusion* has multiple meanings: it means "to bring something to an end," but it also means "to arrive at a judgment." Either way, a conclusion requires our attention and intention.

Conclusions create the intentional rhythms that allow us to experience the life God has made available to us—whether we have just blasted through the ribbon at the finish line of a race or we have quietly come to the end of our rope. Endings get our attention.

In fact, this is not a new idea. A really smart guy already wrote about the importance of endings, and he said they could be even better than beginnings.

The wisest man who ever lived, King Solomon, wrote this in his journal: "Better is the end of a thing than its beginning" (Eccles. 7:8 ESV).

I think we can nod and agree, at least at first. But why?

Of course the end is better than the beginning if the season is hard. We are relieved because it's over, obviously.

But what if a season has been good? Why should it end? How is that ending better than its beginning?

The end is better than the beginning not because it was good or bad but because it happened at all—not because the season is over but because the season *matters*.

God is a masterful storyteller. He is doing something in every moment, and when we learn to create conclusions between seasons, episodes, moments, and happenings, we can see our lives as a story he is telling.

Conclusions are intentional points in time that we create to gain perspective. There is a discipline in this, and it requires a stopping point. An end. A finish line—even a finish line in the messy middle. It doesn't mean the journey is over or has come to an organic finish; it means we must create a point in time to stop and see. We need to create a disruption to the continuation that allows the past to drive our future.

I am a future guy, a visionary. I am always tinkering with ideas, always longing to move forward, to explore, and to see what is possible and available. While that tendency is built into my personality and my work, I have learned that life happens in the present.

God's purposes aren't defined by my plans, my intentions, or my big ideas. He's not hiding in the future, waiting for me in the next episode. He is here now, in this moment, and his plans are fulfilled as my life becomes a part of his story.

His story is not a story of accomplishment but one of redemption, bringing moments to a conclusion with a purpose.

When we learn the power of conclusion, we begin to see how our lives become useful for God's purpose and fulfillment according to his promise. ✱

PART ONE

HOPE COMES IN THE BEGINNING

Hope often couples with excitement, and these emotions swell at the start of something new. But they are a fragile pair, easily choked out, often strangled by the pace and pressure of the process.

Excitement fades to dread and cynicism. Hope loses the battle against futility. We must hold on to hope with both hands. Don't let it slip away.

Hope held is hope renewed, the fuel for endurance on the journey ahead.

CHAPTER 1

"LET'S GO!"

The Hope of Beginnings

"LET'S GO!"

This rally cry means we're off. We're on a new adventure, stepping into a new moment. "Let's go" is our invitation to begin. We love beginnings.

Beginnings have allure. They beckon us forward, they call us ahead, and they draw us from where we are. Beginnings are fun and enticing, a call for celebration. When you're just getting started, anything seems possible. That's the simple beauty of the beginning.

Let's think about this.

When you start a new job, you go out and celebrate with friends. When you have a great first date, you go home with a smile on your face, and your mind races with the possibility of what lies ahead.

When you rent your first apartment or purchase your first home, you might sense an overwhelming feeling of

satisfaction that you are on your own. You have indepen-
dence. You can hang pictures where you want—or don't if
you'd rather not. You can put a bicycle in the living room or
a new TV. (I hung surfboards in my living room for about
five years.)

After all, it's your beginning, in your new place.

If you're a runner, you know that the beginning of a
marathon starts with the fanfare of cheering and a starter
pistol, of crowds and momentum and excitement. The party
at the starting line of a race is exhilarating. At the start,
everything is in front of you, and everything seems possible.

What Is Uniquely Available in the Beginning?

At the starting line, that emotion we feel is actually
hope. We don't initially recognize it by that name because it
looks and feels like excitement, the jitters, or the butterflies.
But deep down, what we feel is something of much greater
consequence.

Deep down, there is a desire and a longing. In this beginning, where everything is in front of us, there is a powerful,
available hope. At its essence, hope is a desire that what we
start will turn out well.

We hope the first date will lead to a great relationship.
We hope this race will provide a sense of conquest or accomplishment. We hope buying the house will prove to be a good
investment and a place filled with incredible memories. We

hope our jobs will be satisfying and our careers will be successful. A beginning is a blank slate for a beautiful, hopeful future.

Beyond Beginning to an Encounter

I live by the ocean. It is a tough life, but someone has to do it.

I try never to take this gift for granted. To keep my appreciation fresh, I often drive down to the beach just to put my feet in the sand. Having grown up in Atlanta, I was landlocked for twenty-one years. The only way to watch the waves was to save our vacation money and drive seven hours to the ocean once a year. Now that it's only a ten-minute drive, I take full advantage of it.

One of my favorite things to do is watch the sunrise. Although, if you think about it, the sun isn't really rising. What is actually happening is even more spectacular. I'm not simply standing still, waiting for the sun to come up. I'm balancing on a rotating rock as it flings through space at about sixty-seven thousand mph, spinning around at a thousand mph. I am waiting to spin far enough to catch the first glimpse of a humongous ball of fire nearly ninety-three million miles away.

Astounding.

We casually call it a sunrise, but I'd say it is a *beautiful* miracle. It's a fresh start, designed and executed by the Maker of the universe, and it happens every single day.

And most mornings we sleep right through it.

Let's clarify: not all beginnings are miraculous, and not everything begins because you wanted it to. Sometimes a beginning starts because you were in the right place at the right time, and sometimes it starts because you are at the wrong place at that time. Sometimes it begins with a peek at something that will become your new reality.

Maybe you didn't plan to start a new season in your life, but you have suddenly found yourself at a new beginning. I call these "encounters," these moments when your life collides with a new reality you had not considered, one you perhaps did not know existed.

I had one of these encounters in the fourth grade. Before that point, my life consisted of an imaginary world of dinosaurs, spaceships, and an occasional visit from Godzilla. At recess my friends Jon, Scotty, and I escaped the demands of the school day to enter our make-believe world and elaborate on the latest time-warp feature on our spaceships. We were invincible, naïve, and absorbed in our own ideas.

Then something *happened*.

After a productive recess, I arrived at my desk to collide with a reality I did not know existed. A note lay on my desk, and I unfolded it to read this:

To: Mike

Dear Mike,
I like you.
Do you like me?

Yes or No

Signed, Jennifer

Here was a question I'd never considered. As far as I recall, the thought of liking a girl had never occurred to me, and now I couldn't get that discovery out of my head.

I tried to ignore it, but it wouldn't go away. Everything in me just wanted to pretend that I hadn't read those words, but it was too late. I'd already collided with this new reality.

No matter how hard I tried, I couldn't get the question out of my mind. I couldn't pretend that I didn't see it. Every time I saw Jennifer, I owed her an answer. The uncertainty of what was happening made we want to avoid her and just retreat to spaceships and dinosaurs.

That is the nature of such an encounter. You didn't plan it or even desire it, but it happened. Most encounters don't arrive as easily as a handwritten note inviting you to circle Yes or No, but there are things that happen that demand our attention and, more importantly, our response.

You have collided with reality. Escape is not an option.

The older we get, the more complicated things become—especially beginnings. You have patterns you've established and people that depend on you. You can't just stop what you're doing to start a new beginning. And yet you can't ignore the encounter.

There are some things you can't unsee. You can't ignore it or shrug it off, even if you try. Once you've seen it, it has invaded your scope of awareness, and you know it's going to make things different. It exists now, and it has your attention.

Fear makes you want it to go away, but hope breathes a different emotion.

Sometimes you can look back and recall the exact moment something began, the second you encountered something new that changed you. These small, unexpected moments can serve as a catalyst for something deeply profound.

Whether it is good news or bad news, this encounter is a collision. You have run into something you can't escape.

Something that changes and shapes you and your future.

Something new has begun, and you must decide how to respond.

You can try to ignore it or wish it away, but it's there now. And it's calling you to make a decision. You have to create a point in time to intentionally deal with the new reality, and this brings you to the conclusion of what has been.

> FEAR MAKES YOU WANT IT TO GO AWAY, BUT HOPE BREATHES A DIFFERENT EMOTION.

A Burning Encounter

Moses experienced an encounter he didn't ask for, one that called him to a brand-new beginning. This is recorded for us in the second book of the Bible, called Exodus. As an Israelite baby, he had been adopted by the Pharaoh's daughter and had grown up in Pharaoh's household with all the royal privileges and amenities of the most powerful family in the world. But the freedom he enjoyed was built on the backs of Israelite slaves, the people of his own flesh and blood. Overcome with rage over how the Egyptian slave masters treated the Israelite slaves, he took justice into his own hands and killed a violent Egyptian soldier.

Afraid that Pharaoh would find out what he had done, Moses ran for his life into the wilderness. He lived in the desert and tended sheep for a long time. He found a wife, together they had children, and he established an anonymous life as a shepherd.

I imagine Moses was familiar with his routines and maybe even comfortably content with his quiet life. He was likely not planning on a new challenge. But when Moses was eighty years old, after forty years as a shepherd in the desert, God suddenly appeared to him in a burning bush. In that moment Moses encountered God, who charged him to go back to Egypt to lead the Israelite slaves to freedom.

I imagine there were moments when Moses wished he had never noticed that fire in the desert. He probably wished he had taken a different route with his sheep that afternoon, and he probably longed to bypass that whole situation. He even asked God to please send someone else. But it was too late; he had seen the bush, and he was now aware of a new reality.

God met Moses in the middle of an ordinary day, and he called him to a new beginning.

This encounter required Moses to close the circle around the life he knew. He couldn't tend sheep and lead the people out of Egypt at the same time. If he had kept the routines of the life he knew, he would have missed God's calling on his life, and he would have missed knowing God as the Father who cares for and redeems his people.

As the sun rose on Moses' new beginning, the sun set on the old reality he had known.

Like Moses, you might wish to look the other way. You might long to ignore what you have encountered, and you might wish to pretend you don't know what you know. But this moment matters. You have collided with something new. A new beginning calls for an ending, and conclusions can be difficult when they call us to embrace the end of the way things were.

If you don't conclude the moments that have come before, you could miss knowing God in the moments to come.

God Does Not Write Fairy Tales

The fairy tales we love most open in a classic voice: "Once upon a time."

Those words signal the start of a story. They jump-start a journey into the deepest parts of what we want. We keep spinning stories and weaving tales, and we step in as witnesses to the action and the drama, the fairy-tale ball, the beautiful dress, the slain dragons, the defeated villains, and the triumph of all that is good. We get to feel the tension, and we get to celebrate the resolve.

Here's the thing about fairy tales, though: we can't contribute.

While we can feel emotionally involved, while we cheer for the heroes and boo at the villains, we aren't actually living the story. We're spectators. Even if we're as close as the front row, we're still only watching the story. We aren't in the story.

That's where God's story is different. God does not write fairy tales.

His story has all the common elements of a fairy tale (or rather, fairy tales commonly reflect elements of God's story), with this one wonderful difference: his story is true, and we are invited to participate in it.

"Once upon a time" introduces us to what has already happened to someone else. The story of God opens differently. The Bible opens with the words, "In the beginning."

This story isn't only about what has happened but what is *happening*.

The story that unfolds in the Bible isn't about another time and another place. This story reveals the heart of God inviting us into his work and his purpose. He has created us to participate with him in what he is creating.

We read, "In the beginning," and the sentence continues: "God created."

This line sweeps everything into the voice of the Creator, inviting us to bring everything we have received into his epic story. Our voice, our choices, our decisions, and our lives contribute to the saga of a glorious God through his glorious creation.

When God initiated all of creation, forming everything that surrounds us, he did not simply get the ball rolling and then wait to see where it went. Even at the beginning, we were part of what he started, and he wanted us in the story with him. "In the beginning" isn't an invitation to watch from the sidelines. It's a call to contribute, to participate, to join in, to live the story.

> OUR VOICE, OUR CHOICES, OUR DECISIONS, AND OUR LIVES CONTRIBUTE TO THE SAGA OF A GLORIOUS GOD THROUGH HIS GLORIOUS CREATION.

Every choice we make contributes to our character development and to the arc of our story, and because we know the Author, we can trust that every stroke of the story is infused with hope. Hope is the thing that compels us to risk the unknown and to endure on the path, even when we cannot see the way forward. Beginnings draw hope into the light, long middles cause hope to fade, and uncertain endings make hope seem dark; but in God's story, hope is always there. When God launches beginnings, he has the end in mind, both for the sake of what comes after and for the hope of every moment in between.

A beginning must have a conclusion, and even a short story must have an ending—that's what makes it a story. In this story God is writing, we live between the epic beginning and the epic end. God pours forth his speech one day at a time, and our story unfolds the same way, under the same promise of hope. There is a day when faith will give way to sight, and hope will no longer be needed because every desire will be fully and finally fulfilled. Every tear will be wiped away and every fear vanished in the thrill of the final redemption of all things.

Beginnings might be easy, but the conclusion is where you'll see what you're longing for.

This season, this day, this moment as you read this page—this is your small start. You've picked up this book and started a journey. Maybe you're not even normally a reader, so I'd like to congratulate you on what you've already done by reading these few pages.

Now, if you are like me, you may get about one-third of the way through the book and start to feel the pressure to finish. You'll flip through the pages in your right hand, look to see how much is left, and maybe start to think you'll never finish.

But the journey isn't about finishing. Process is everything.

The beauty is in the process because you're only ever in this moment, on the page you're on, living the season of life you're in. Don't miss the thing God is doing in this moment.

This is your beginning, the time and place where you can encounter God on an ordinary day.

Let's go. ✳

CHAPTER 2

GETTING GOING

Getting Started Is Different from Getting Going

HAVE YOU EVER stopped to think about the fact that once upon a time, *there was no time?*

Mind. Blown.

As a kid I could never figure this out. (Frankly, as an adult I still can't figure it out.)

If you stop and think for a minute, time is one of the most interesting concepts. We already have a tendency to think we don't have enough time, so we can't really even fathom the concept of no time at all.

When God created our universe, he invented time. He could have designed us so that we were each born with a watch on our wrist, but instead he created an intricate design to mark the passing of time.

He put a large light in the sky to govern the day, and he put a lesser light in the sky to govern the night (Gen. 1:16). He created a giant ball of fire in the universe, and he surrounded it with rocks that would circulate around it, thereby creating days, weeks, months, seasons, and years, each with a beginning and an end.

I live near the beach in North Carolina, in an area that has basically one season. I mean, it's not as uniform as Florida or Southern California because we do have winter. It runs for about a month, from mid-January to the third week of February. At the end of February, the temperature hits 75 degrees for about two weeks, and we call that spring. After that, it's summer again until Thanksgiving.

This works for me because I love summer, but I have learned that most people love seasons. They like to have a distinct spring, summer, winter, and fall. And I understand that. It can be disorienting when it's 85 degrees and sunny in December, and it's weird to play Christmas carols in short sleeves. You can't really tell where a thing begins if it just perpetually continues, one season into the next without a conclusion of the one before.

Each day has twenty-four hours, a span of time we often wish we could stretch even longer to hold even more, but each day comes to an end so a new one can begin. Spring follows winter, but—more than that—the beginning of spring marks the end of winter. Seasons consist of beginnings and endings, a rhythm for the transition of old things to new.

Time is the only constant in all of our lives, and it can either blur or stand still.

There's a relationship between hope and time; when we feel hopeless, time seems to multiply itself in an endless loop of discouragement. But when we feel hopeful, time offers possibility. All of the uncertainty that once felt so heavy is now pregnant with possibility.

Most of us think of time as a linear concept, that it starts at one point on a line and runs indefinitely in the same direction. Time keeps ticking into the future, always moving forward.

That is true, but we also think it's something we can invest or spend.

We say things like, "Time is money!" That's an American phrase, a Western way of thinking, and it's a myth. Time is not money. You can accumulate five-dollar bills, ten-dollar bills, or if you're really lucky, you might even get a few one-hundred-dollar bills. But time does not work this way.

You receive time one second at a time. You can't get different denominations. Time comes to you in the same amount, every single time. You can't multiply it, and you can't invest it wisely so you can get more. There is no compounding interest. It comes at you with exact precision.

If you think time is money, you will devalue anything and everything that does not add monetary value to your life. If you feel like you are wasting time, then you will feel like you're wasting your wealth and, therefore, your life. This mentality will keep you from valuing the truly important things.

We also say things like this: "Time heals." Another myth. Time doesn't heal. Time is a carrier of grace, and grace has the power to heal, but the time itself doesn't heal. It just keeps on ticking into the future. Time isn't money, and time doesn't heal.

Perhaps there is another way of thinking about this.

Time and grace are like oxygen: we receive them in the moment we are in. We cannot save them or store them to use later when we might need more. You may get really efficient at "managing your time," but you cannot actually move time around on the calendar.

You cannot hold your breath and store it away for a time when you'll expect to need a deeper inhale. You can only take one breath at a time, and you can only live one moment at a time. When each breath is concluded, you trust there will be more air in the next moment.

Grace is also this way: we do not store it away for moments to come. We live in the grace we have right now, with hope and trust that God will give us enough for the moments to come—moment to moment, grace to grace. Time is the medium through which we experience grace.

In the beginning, we see this incredible picture of God speaking everything into existence. He called forth beauty and life from the fullness of himself, and from that point, everything he has created continues to declare his glory and his grace. From the very start, he created a rhythm of beginnings for us every twenty-four hours.

Imagine if you were there, if you could have witnessed this epic beginning. You hear a voice thundering, "Let there be light," and the darkness gives way. Imagine the picture of light pushing back the darkness is embedded in the rhythm of creation, this miracle of the sunrise.

The miracle is not only an astrological wonder of a ball of fire and rocks spinning through space. The miracle is that every single day begins with the reminder that life and full-ness flow from him, and these are available to us every day.

It is one thing to see the beauty of a sunrise, and it is another to hear the promise of the miraculous beginning of a new day dawning.

The darkness is necessary for the light to rise. The end of a thing is necessary for the beginning of another, the start of the new. And when the shadows of the past over-whelm us, when what we can glimpse of the future makes us fearful, we need to know what is available now. God's promise can bring hope in the moment when most every-thing seems hopeless.

This miracle is a reminder that something is available. The prophet Jeremiah paints this beautiful picture in his lament over his disappointment with the way things have gone.

Let's join him on the edge of the sunrise, just moments from the first light, still surrounded by the uncertainty of the dark. This is what Jeremiah records:

> "My soul is downcast within me. Yet this I call
> to mind and therefore I have hope." (Lam.
> 3:20–21

He feels the weight of the world. His heart is broken and his mind is frazzled. You've been there, too: disappointed, frustrated, angry, wondering what is the point, and where is the hope?

Though we want to escape these emotions, run from them, or numb them, we need to follow Jeremiah's example and start by bringing them to the surface. We need to feel the emotions and name them.

But he doesn't stop there. He is reminded of something that brings him hope.

Let's read on:

> "Because of the LORD's great love we are not
> consumed, for his compassions never fail.
> They are new every morning; great is your
> faithfulness." (Lam. 3:22–23)

God's unfailing love—his steadfast, loyal love—holds us and sustains us so we aren't consumed by a broken, disappointed, angry, frazzled threat. His compassion and great love for us never fail.

Here is the picture: they come new and fresh with every sunrise. With the beginning of each ordinary day, God meets us with new morning mercy. It isn't leftover from the day, it isn't a savings account we can tap into, and it isn't a favor to cash in. He comes to us with enough for today, inviting us to receive. The sunrise declares the sufficient, faithful care of God and invites us to trust the grace available in this new moment.

Just as we know the sun will rise, we know God will be faithful to finish what he began (Phil. 1:6).

Don't miss this: trusting his faithfulness is foundational to trusting the process.

We can trust him for what we need, right when we need it.

Don't miss this because you don't have time.

Making Room Is Making Time

"I don't have time."

I have often caught myself using this phrase to avoid doing something. Whether dealing with an annoying situation or a difficult person, "I don't have time" becomes a great excuse.

There is one problem: it isn't a true statement. I do have time. I'd just rather choose to use it on other things. As long as I think I don't have time, I will continue to live at the mercy of the pressure I feel at the expense of the mercy God makes available.

Let's talk about the innkeeper. Every December we talk about this guy when we

TRUSTING HIS FAITHFULNESS IS FOUNDATIONAL TO TRUSTING THE PROCESS.

revisit the story of Jesus' birth. I think we feel like we know him pretty well, but I suspect he'd probably like to rewrite his role in the story of the night Jesus was born.

In Luke chapter 2, we read about the decreed census for the entire Roman world and how Mary and Joseph made the long journey to Bethlehem when she was far along in her pregnancy. "The time came for Mary to give birth to her baby. Her first son was born. She put cloth around Him and laid Him in a place where cattle are fed. There was no room for them in the place where people stay for the night" (vv. 6–7 NLV).

Other versions say: "There was no guest room available for them," or "There was no room in the hostel."

Guest room, hostel, no room in the place where people stay . . . all of these stem from a phrase a lot of us learned when we were children. Mary gave birth to a child, she wrapped him in swaddling clothes, and she laid him in a manger—why?

All together now: "Because there was no room for him in the inn."

That one verse gives the innkeeper a bad rap that has stayed with him for two thousand years. He's the one who wouldn't make room for Jesus.

And so, if you're like me, you may have thought to yourself, *What kind of doofus was the innkeeper, right? Who would do that to Jesus? What was wrong with this guy?*

But maybe there is another explanation.

What if the innkeeper wasn't mean at all, and what if there was just nothing he could do that evening when the young couple knocked at his door? What if his hotel was legitimately full? What if it was already overrun with people? All of a sudden, here come Mary and Joseph, and she's obviously about to give birth, but maybe the guy had no choice.

I picture his wife speaking to him privately in the back office of the inn, saying to him, "Honey, she's *pregnant*! We have to do *something*!" And he was maybe like, "I know, babe, but there's nothing I can do! Do you want to give them *our* bed?"

I began to noodle on this.

Think about what could have happened if the innkeeper had made room for Jesus. I bet you this: if he had made room for Jesus, that hotel would still be in business. Can you imagine the sign out front? *Jesus was born here!* They would never shut it down. Want to talk about "no room at the inn"—that place would be booked for centuries to come.

I allowed my imagination to consider for a moment what it would have been like to be the innkeeper. Sure, maybe he was mean or indifferent, or maybe he was just stressed.

Maybe he didn't have any room in his life for any more decisions.

When I picture this aspect of the innkeeper, a responsible guy with a lot on his mind, I can relate. Maybe the innkeeper is more like us than we think. None of us would intentionally leave Jesus out, right? But the reality is, with all the demands we have on our lives, the pressures we face, and the constant pace of our lives—we don't have room for more: more responsibility, more decisions, or more things we feel like we ought to be doing.

The pressure and the pace leave us no room for rhythm. One moment blurs into the next, one day piles on top of another, the sun rises, the sun sets, and we don't even notice. We miss the whisper of the new morning mercy.

So, how do we make room for Jesus? You make room by making time.

In the youth ministry where I grew up, I heard this phrase over and over again: "If you're too busy to spend time with God, then you are busier than he intends for you to be."

If I were you, I would probably stop and write that down and put it somewhere you can see it.

Every time my pace gets to a breakneck speed, when I begin to think I don't have time for God, I am confronted with that truth: I am busier than he intends for me to be. The solution is not to feel bad or to promise to do better.

HOW DO WE MAKE ROOM FOR JESUS? YOU MAKE ROOM BY MAKING TIME.

The solution is to make room by making time. There is no substitute for this. We will only find God's purpose and perspective in His presence. ✳

CHAPTER 3

HOLDING HOPE

Conclusions Allow You to Live in the Now

MY MOVIE TASTE is very narrow. I enjoy Christmas movies and animated features, and that's pretty much it. I could make a strong argument that the movie *Elf* is one of the greatest Christmas movies of all time. Will Ferrell plays an elf named Buddy. Only he isn't actually an elf; he's a human who was raised by elves when he accidentally arrived at the North Pole as a baby. When Buddy learns he's not a real elf, he goes on an adventure to New York City to connect with his biological father—who (a) has no idea Buddy exists and (b) is on the Naughty List for a lifetime of bad choices. Christmas spirit is on the line.

(If you haven't seen *Elf*, you should. Naturally, don't watch it for a lesson in theology. But do watch it for some of the best one-liners in Christmas movie history.)

There's a scene when Buddy gets banished to the mail room at his dad's publishing company, and he turns the place into a dance club. He has a little too much "syrup" with his new friend, and the two of them are lying back on a pile of mail, talking about going with the flow.

The guy laments that, at his age (twenty-six), he should've accomplished more with his life. It's somewhat of a joke since we can all look at the guy and see he's long past twenty-six. I did a little research and discovered that the actor was approximately forty-six when the movie was released.[2] I love the brilliance of the casting, to show that the guy feels so much older than he is.

I talk to people in this stage of life all the time, people in their mid-twenties and early thirties who believe they should be further along than they are. They always say, "I should have done more by now."

I always ask the question, "What do you think you should have done?"

Their answer is always the same: "I don't know."

How is it that you should have done more if you don't know what you should have done? It's an illusion. We have this preconceived idea that we should be at a certain place by a certain date in our lives, especially those who are thirty-five and under.

This is a habit that I call Destination Thinking.

Destination Thinking is the pattern that says, "When I get out of this season, everything will be better." We tell ourselves everything will be better when I get out of high school. Then it will be better when I am finally in college. Then it will be better when I get married. Then it will be better when we have kids. Then when the kids are grown. It is an endlessly moving destination you're trying to reach. Turns out, you can never really reach it. The destination is a mirage.

This journey leaves us chasing the future and increasing the pressure on our present with each unsatisfying season. Hope gives way to demand, and we then put pressure on everything else. This is the curse of continuation.

Goal setting and a performance-driven lifestyle can trap us into this mindset. We can even spiritualize it by setting formative goals that will make us better people, make us better Christians, make us better at life if we can just reach that destination. Our tendency is to get out of what we're in, to push through to a new beginning. But that's not necessarily formative. Sometimes it's just escape.

The end of a thing is better than the beginning but not simply because it's behind us. The ending is better because it gives birth to a new thing. We don't escape the old things; we find purpose in them. Endings and beginnings give rhythm to what God is actually doing.

The Tension of the Faster

"If I can just get through this, then everything will be okay." Have you ever said that to yourself? I feel like I've been saying that since 2012.

The list of things to get through becomes longer and longer. The only solution to this increasing demand is to pick up the pace, to go faster and faster. Before you know it, you're disconnected from everything and everyone that matters to you. The faster you go, the more things blur. You can't see clearly in a hurry.

When your only sense of pace is "faster," you lose the thing you need to gain understanding: perspective.

Your pace prevents perspective.

In 2007, my one word was *finish*. I picked that word because I wanted to be better at finishing tasks. Things were moving fast and furious in my life, and I didn't like the feeling of tasks undone. I wanted to be better at finishing my messages, the articles I needed to write, the emails I needed to respond to, the books I was reading—all of it. I wanted to finish.

YOU CAN'T SEE CLEARLY IN A HURRY.

In retrospect, I got really good at finishing. I'd finish my tasks, finish my lists, and feel a general sense of accomplishment in my workday.

And then I'd come home *exhausted*.

My kids were small then, and they were excited for their evenings with dad, but I was so tired. I'd say, "Kids, let's see how fast we can do our baths and bedtime stories to see who can get into bed first. Ready? Go!"

Have you ever raced your kids to bed?

Obviously, you don't do this because you're trying to make memories. You do it because you're trying to get them out of your hair. Because they'll take up more energy than you have.

Why was I in such a hurry?

I'll tell you why: I was in a hurry to get in my recliner so I could watch ESPN, while I relaxed in my shorts and black socks. (For some reason, that was the picture of adulthood for me: watching TV in my own home, wearing shorts and black socks.) I was racing my kids to bed so I could get into that ridiculous position that felt like winning to me.

Reality hit me like a freight train when I realized the pattern I had created. I had finished my workday at five, but I wasn't truly finished with my day at all. My little girls were growing up, and their dad was rushing through their childhood, all in an effort to get through.

It was midyear when I realized this. This is one of the great things about choosing one word: the focus you begin the year with usually doesn't last through the end. The perspective shifts, and you have to shift with it to understand what you're seeing. Six months in, I began to think about what it could look like to finish the day *well*, to actually finish the day by being present with my family. Instead of just drifting off into a coma at the end of the day, maybe I could actually go to sleep knowing I had finished well.

For many of us, time seems to barrel forward. Like a snowball down a hill, collecting more and more stuff and

getting bigger and bigger until our lives feel like an avalanche rushing out of control and overtaking everything.
Nothing's finished, and all of our problems and struggles—
even our successes—just seem to be one continuous drive
forward into the future. This creates an unsustainable constant that drives us mad.

Rick Warren said, "Nobody pressures you without your
permission."[3] That's a freeing idea: nothing has the power to
pressure me unless I allow it. But without perspective, things
pile up and put pressure on us without our permission. We
feel buried beneath that list of the things we should have
done if we were really the people we hoped to be.

We feel so much pressure when we are not accomplish-
ing things as fast as we want to or when things aren't going
as we had hoped they would. The result is perpetual frustration. As the future gets closer, the more pressure we feel.
This is why we wake up feeling crushed under the weight of
a new day. We have so much to get done before the future
gets here.

The undone creates pressure, and it's not just the
undone, it's the uncertainty. We've got so much to do, and
we don't necessarily know what it is.

As adults, we don't know what we should have done, but
we do know that it's more than what we're currently doing.
So we ramp up. We want our kids to do better than we did, so
we put pressure on them to do more than we've done, even
though we're not sure what that is. We're just piling more

pressure on, more and more, from one generation to the next, creating a crushing burden no one can bear.

We look at all that needs to be done, and we think there are only two categories: do everything, or do nothing. But there is a third option: do the things we are suppose to, in order to become the person we are created to be. Instead of rushing to do it all, we need to stop to ask if the things we're doing are things we should be doing.

We need to stop and ask ourselves: Did this begin with a choice? Did I make an intentional choice to follow God's invitation in the moment, or did I get swept into the pressure to hurry? When we hurry, we begin to do things we don't notice, and we do things we never intended.

Hurry is the enemy of the heart and deep character change. We have created an entire industry devoted to this enemy of peace and sanity. We call it hustle, and we make it sound heroic. But hustle is just one more way for the continuation of our past to pile up and the continuation of the pressure we feel about the coming future. This is a recipe for an implosion.

Hurry isn't just about pace; it is about pressure. Dallas Willard wrote extensively about this, proposing that hurry is the great enemy of spiritual life in our day. He said we must "ruthlessly eliminate hurry."[4] We have got to get out from under the pressure, and we do that by disrupting the continuation and drawing a conclusion. This is how we establish once again the rhythms in which God has invited us to live.

Jesus was never in a hurry. As Jesus became more and more popular, he was wanted all over the place. He was actually the only one who *could* have done all the things he was asked to do, but he modeled for us this unhurried way of life. His disciples were rushing him from one appointment to the next, trying to stay on top of his schedule. I picture them calling ahead on their phones, making sure reservations are in place. And then Jesus would throw off their entire schedule when he stopped to speak to two blind men. I wonder how often we miss the things God has for us simply because we are trying so hard to get to where we think we ought to be.

We all know the pressure to impress or to be perceived as productive. A friend of Jesus knew this pressure well. Martha was known as "the one who could get it done." If there's a to-do list, she'll conquer it. Jesus was coming for lunch, and her image was on the line. Her motives were not bad, and neither are ours, necessarily. But when we get rushed, we forget what is important.

Jesus shows up to her house for lunch, and Martha is busily rushing around to complete the details while her sister Mary sits down with Jesus. Martha is busy hosting, and Mary is not busy at all. Martha has had enough.

I imagine Martha trying to make eye contact with Mary, getting her to clear the dishes, but Mary misses her hints. Martha is furious; Mary is oblivious. Luke records that Martha was distracted with so much serving, but Mary was focused, fully present.

Finally, Martha leans on her last resort: she drags Jesus right into her feud with her sister. I'm not sure there's a worse place to be than stuck in a spat between two sisters. "Lord, do you not care that my sister has left me to serve alone? Tell her then to help me" (Luke 10:40 ESV).

Massive assumption. She assumed Jesus agreed with her, and she told him to correct her sister. Jesus responds to Martha, and perhaps this is his response to you, "You are anxious and troubled about many things, but one thing is necessary" (vv. 40–42).

Jesus seems to want her to make room for him. (Take that, innkeeper.)

There's nothing more important than an encounter with Jesus. How often are we so anxious and troubled about so many things that we neglect the one thing that is necessary in order for everything else to find its place and purpose?

Productivity has become our default measure of success. So many of us are overwhelmed by the goal of productivity, and insecurity runs rampant when we can't rattle off an impressive list of the things we have produced in a given day—or by the time we turn thirty-five. We deceive ourselves with thoughts like, *If I had produced more, then I would be more. If I had been more competitive, I would be more. If I had accomplished more, if I had a better resume. If I had more income, if I had more meetings, if I had a better sense of identity—then I would be more.* These are examples of destination thinking, and they are simply untrue. They keep us continually chasing, and therefore they keep us from being still and making room for Jesus.

To Do or to Be

From time to time, I have the privilege to lead corporate events, usually centered around the concept of My One Word. One of the questions I often begin with is, "How many people in the room make to-do lists?"

Hands shoot up. People love their to-do lists.

The group of Type A go-getters love the idea of getting stuff done. The show of hands is usually accompanied by some chatter about Post-it Notes, digital versus paper, and other performance hacks they've discovered.

Then I ask a follow-up question: "You have to-do lists. How many have a to-be list?'

Crickets.

No one says anything. I have even seen tears.

Because we spend so much effort on getting things done and because we weigh our identity against our productivity, we end up disappointed with whom we've become in the process.

We all know that who we are becoming is far more important than what we've accomplished, but we don't live like we know it. We need a way to see this and pursue it. We need to understand that who we are becoming is not something we do or achieve or cross off a list. The way we experience the time we have and what we do with the way we encounter our circumstances—this is what will shape us.

We feel such pressure to *do* that we end up addicted to beginnings, just to stay in motion. If we are not intentional, we can let our starts pile up, one after another, simply because we like to feel hopeful and accomplished. Starts give the illusion of accomplishment, so when we feel discouraged, we simply start something new. That escape undermines our willingness to endure.

When we get bogged down in uncertainty, we avoid finishing things. We just push ahead to another beginning. Too often we deal with a threat of a dashed hope by running ahead into the future. This perpetuates the pressure.

As someone who is prone to chase shiny objects, I know the appeal of a starting line. It is easier to look for other starting lines than to stick around when it gets hard. Continuation likes to mask itself as a series of chronic beginnings.

The excitement of beginnings can mask the disappointment of the past as the thrill of something new drowns out the pain of the previous season. This is why some of us jump out of one relationship and into a new one, why we start a new job when the last one gets difficult. We avoid pain by jumping from new thing to new thing, and we completely bypass the process of formation. We create binge experiences that keep us bouncing from thing to thing, faster and faster.

This disjointed rhythm blurs our perspective, whether we are escaping the regret of the past or the pressure of the future.

The disappointments and mistakes of yesterday don't go away because we continued into a new day. They don't fade with the sunset or disappear with the sunrise. Remember, time doesn't really heal. If we leave these things untended, disappointment and pain begin to pile up. We end up dragging the baggage of the past into the future, chasing a destination we think will finally fulfill the hope we have and bring the healing we need. It will not.

To make room for Jesus is an invitation to stay the course. Staying the course has its own danger, though, as we create winning streaks we feel we must maintain. ✳

CHAPTER 4

PRESSURE TO CONTINUE

Winning Streaks Are Not Finish Lines

In 1978, I was sitting in the living room with my family watching the Atlanta Braves play the Cincinnati Reds, a common custom for my family when I was young. This particular game stood out for two reasons. First, Gene Garber was pitching for Atlanta, and I loved his style when he threw the ball—he pitched side armed, almost underhanded. His fingers looked like they might graze the dirt on his follow-through.

The second reason is a bit more significant in the records of sports history: Pete Rose, the great hitter for the Cincinnati Reds, was on a forty-four-game hitting streak. For non-baseball fans, that means he had hit the ball and got on base in forty-four straight games. We were in the ninth inning, and he had yet to have a hit. His forty-four-game hitting streak was in jeopardy.

Rose stepped to the plate to a roaring ovation—even though they were playing in Atlanta. Home-field advantage had nothing on his fan base. The commentators were rambling on and on about the streak while at the same time arguing about the need not to think about it. In other words, the talkers were talking about how they shouldn't be talking about the things they were talking about. It was just a normal at bat, they said, as they talked about the history he could make if he got a hit.

The threat of failure piled onto the pressure, making it anything but normal. History was on the line. It had been forty-four games since he'd gone hitless, and now the threat of the streak coming to an end loomed large, as did the opportunity to set a new record.

This moment was packed with potential for either the thrill of victory or the agony of defeat. The pressure of the moment and the utter ordinariness of the moment—an at bat just like he'd done a thousand times—all compressed in the same space.

On that night, Pete Rose's forty-four-game hitting streak came to an end. Gene Garber struck him out. There was a giant exhale across the land, and things went back to normal in the world of baseball. All streaks come to an end.

Streaks create pressure in all the wrong places. We end up paying attention to the wrong things, and then we try to pretend we aren't paying attention to them.

We should take the time to ask ourselves, though, What is the value of a streak? It is simply a series of choices, a pattern of moments. We deceive ourselves when we begin to think we are on a trajectory of where we have always been, whether that means forever adding to a win or forever doomed to lose.

We have to take the pressure off the streak without devaluing the choice in the moment.

Measuring the Wrong Metrics

I spent a lot of years being crazy competitive, driven by a need to prove myself. Losing felt like an indictment against me, so the only option was to win. I had a lot of unhealthy rhythms, and I could not rest. I felt pressure, and that caused me to focus on performance. When I got home at night, I felt like I still needed to be productive, always looking for the next hill, the next conquest.

When we're always chasing, we start comparing ourselves to everyone else. We start competing in everything. Every industry has its score card contributing to this kind of pressure. Real estate transactions, Amazon reviews, ticket sales—increasing numbers indicate success, and unfortunately ministry is no exception.

When I first started in youth ministry, the unspoken rule was that a thriving youth group needed to have at least one hundred students. That was the goal I needed to meet if I was worth my salt as a youth pastor. I kept an eye on other youth groups in the area, and I wanted to compete with their attendance. It was as if leading a youth group was a contest to win, a sport to conquer. I wanted our weekly numbers to go up and up and up.

I remember when I realized how toxic that had become. I knew it wasn't what God wanted for our youth group, and it wasn't what God wanted for me. And if I didn't do something to address these expectations, this pattern would likely continue. Each week's attendance had to be better than the one before, but when we treat spiritual development like a sport to win, there's no room for relationships, no room for real growth.

We don't often stop and consider what we are looking for because of the pressure we feel to continue with what we've always done. We tend to count the ways we've always counted, using the same scorecard we've always used. Hitting your sales goals, increased revenue, the size of your church, square footage of your house, zeroes in your bank account—all of these build pressure to maintain habits that are hard to break. Even now, friendships are measured by the streaks on social media, and academics are measured by perfect attendance. (Who wants that award? Can't you play hooky, just once?)

When we run unchecked, these increasing numbers become our source of hope, and decreasing numbers become the plague of disappointment. When the numbers go the wrong way, we don't come up with a new score card. We work harder to turn the numbers around, and we get worn out, burned out, and consumed by the wrong things.

The Deception of Spiritual Winning Streaks

Years ago, I was a New Year's resolution freak. Out of the hundreds I have made, I only vividly recall two of them: to stop drinking soft drinks and to run a marathon. Why did those two stand out? Because one is still undone and the other is still in tact.

I haven't had a soft drink since December 31, 1999. It's been 8,128 days (and counting) since I've had a Coke. You could say I'm on a streak. (I have no desire to run a marathon—not sure what I was thinking.)

You probably have a streak, too. In the absence of any other way to measure growth, we really don't have a choice. Consider questions like, "How long has it been since you've had a drink? A smoke? Lost your temper? Said a bad word?" We give answers to these questions in measurements of time. That's how we know when we're stuck on the streak.

Or maybe, instead of measuring how long it's been since we did something bad, we might keep track of how many consecutive times we were able to do something good. You might rejoice over doing your daily devotions for twenty-seven days straight. Or you might feel proud for attending church every Sunday for the last three years. You have volunteered at the homeless shelter every month for five years. You've got habits, structure, and momentum in place, and you're feeling great about this streak.

If you have a few days under you, then you start to feel really good about yourself, right? You look in the mirror, stand up a little taller, and give yourself a pat on the back for doing such a good job at "being good." We start to feel confident about getting that sin under control.

Or, we might begin to feel trapped by the streak. I've done this for so long, what happens now if I stop?

And then the inevitable happens. After twenty-one days, you lost your temper. You had a drink. You cussed in front of the kids. You ate too much pizza. You did the best you could for as long as you could, and then—WHAM! You fell off the wagon. You blew it.

All hope feels lost when you have broken the streak.

Our prayers sound like this: "I can't believe I did that. I'm such a failure. Sorry, God. I won't let it happen again. I promise I won't let you down again." That promise only begins a new streak—with shame piled on top of it.

That's why we can't live like this. When you measure your life in streaks, one mistake feels like all your hard work has come crashing down. One misstep, and we think it's all been for nothing, that we're right back where we started.

But we're not. We just had a bad day.

Good Days and Bad Days

Was it really a bad day, though? See, we generally have two files where we store our days: the Good Day File and the Bad Day File. If you ask anyone how their day was, they can tell you which file the day goes in: Good Day or Bad Day. Sometimes we even round down and call it a Terrible Day. Ask why it was a terrible day, and it's usually the result of a terrible five minutes. It could have been a perfect day, but then you hit traffic on your way home. Or you got home and discovered your kids left their breakfast dishes in the sink. Five bad minutes can tip the scales.

It's pretty impressive how much power we give to five minutes of a day. There are 1,440 minutes in a day, so percentage wise, five minutes is only 0.003 percent of any given day. It's a pretty short streak, and yet we are willing to toss the whole day into the Bad Day File.

A while back, I began to notice that I had like four bad days for each one of my good days. That's not a healthy rhythm. We need a better way to process our days rather than a binary pendulum of black and white, good and bad, one or the other, all or nothing.

IT'S PRETTY IMPRESSIVE HOW MUCH POWER WE GIVE TO FIVE MINUTES OF A DAY.

Here's the question: What is the ratio? How many good days are enough? How long is long enough? When will you ever do enough to live up to the standard you're convinced

God expects from you, or that someone in your life expects from you, or that you expect from yourself?

God invites us to change our thinking with a fresh mindset: *number every single day*. Psalm 90:12 says, "Teach us to number our days, that we may present to you a heart of wisdom" (NASB).

There are two essential pieces here to consider. First, this is a perspective we have to be taught. It's not a natural way of seeing life. Second, there's an action here, something to *do*. It's not an empty promise or a vague goal, to just "be better." The task is to actually count our days. He does not mean to add them up in order to build a streak but to assign weight to them.

This day—this one, today's date on the calendar, the one you and I are each living—will serve a purpose. The purpose has nothing to do with our success, accomplishments, performance, or what people think about us. It has everything to do with this place inside us, where we are each accountable for the condition of our heart.

Instead of assessing each day as Good or Bad, we can conclude each day as important. As we do, God will be faithful to finish what he started. Trusting his faithfulness is foundational to trusting the process.

Go ahead and write that down again. I'll wait.

We must give an account to God. This doesn't just happen at the end of life, with one giant finish line of a life well lived. This accounting happens every day, as we answer for the small choices that reflect our character, our integrity, and our love for people.

Make time in the morning to remember that *this day* counts, so you can remember throughout the day that *each moment* counts. If the five minutes that derailed an entire day can receive such disproportionate weight, imagine the exponential power of one faithful moment. ✳

PART TWO

ENDURANCE BEGINS

Endurance begins with grace *in* the moment. This section emphasizes our decisions and actions in the moment to break the pileup of our past and to awaken hope for our future.

When you finally decide the streaks don't matter, you can endure the process by living in the moment.

CHAPTER 5

EVERY MOMENT MATTERS

Making the Process a Priority

MY WIFE IS the queen of baby steps and the ten-minute tidy, of conquering large tasks through the momentum of short goals. When a task seems too big to tackle, when the condition of the house seems too overwhelming, Julie has taught our family to set a timer and commit to ten minutes of tidying. "Hey guys, let's see how much we can get done in ten minutes," she'll say. That's all. Just ten minutes.

If you say to your kids, "This (bedroom, playroom, garage, basement, etc.) is a disaster zone. We have to get it clean today, no matter how long it takes," then you've set yourselves up for a day of arguing, begging, pleading, negotiating, and very little cleaning. When there's no end in sight, being overwhelmed turns into hopelessness and then into paralysis. Enter the ten-minute tidy!

At first, it might sound too simple and cheesy. It might even sound like a disingenuous motivation tactic to get your kids (or your spouse) to get stuff done, and in some ways it is a kind of bait and switch. You are trading the feeling of futility for the joy of empowerment, the endless overwhelm of a thousand miles for the measure of taking a short step. It's truly a powerful approach to simply enter into the moment in front of you. Your momentum may even compel you to start the timer again, and before you know it, you'll have reset the timer four times and find you've been crazy productive—and the project only took you forty minutes instead of four hours.

Here's a little confession: I actually use a timer for both my reading and my writing because I'm not super great at either. I can get distracted and off task if I let my mind wander, but I have found I can read for ten minutes without stopping. The same is true for writing. I am amazed at how much progress I can make, just ten minutes at a time.

The truth is, everybody can do something for ten minutes, and when the timer rings, your momentum will often compel you to start it again. Something about knowing you've got a small, achievable goal lets you dive all the way in. Then, once you're immersed, you want to keep going. Before you know it, ten minutes has turned into forty minutes, and you've made so much progress.

Sometimes it's bigger than a messy garage, a cluttered basement, or writing a chapter of a book. Sometimes it's the magnitude of life itself that overwhelms us. This is when we make sweeping statements like, "Nothing is working!

Everything has come apart! It's ruined. Nothing will ever be good again."

We look at all that we have to do, all that is expected of us, all that is out of whack, and we conclude that the only real options are to lay on the couch, binge some TV, or start drinking. When our world is a disaster zone and we can't do anything until it all gets cleaned up, it's tempting to throw our hands in the air and resolve that nothing can be done.

We live in a world that celebrates progress, not process. Progress has become the golden calf. We put disproportionate weight on the giant finish line, as if it is everything. If the goal is "everything," then anything else is "nothing." We tell ourselves the process holds no value, when in fact it was the rhythm of the "ten-minute

PROGRESS HAS BECOME THE GOLDEN CALF.

tidy" that got us to the goal. It was the small finish lines along the way that gave us the endurance to finish.

Time is both a measurement of progress and a medium for process. When we set the timer and work hard for ten minutes, we're using time to measure our progress. But in those ten minutes, something else is happening—to us and in us.

Every moment in this journey matters. Disney has figured this out.

Finding Meaning in the Journey

In my family, we are huge fans of Disney, and even just writing the word *Disney* makes me want to drop everything and go back. We've done that trip basically every way you can do it, and we have gotten there almost every way you can go. We know that driving takes almost fifteen hours, and if you push through, it turns into the longest day of your life. You're tired and miserable when you get there, and you can almost ruin an entire vacation because of the fatigue of the travel. It's a rough start when the travel itself is something you have to suffer through.

But the folks at Disney have figured this out. They have designed a process that turns the travel into a meaningful journey of its own. Your Disney *experience*—far more than a vacation—begins long before you arrive at the park, even long before the day you leave your house.

About a month before your trip, the Disney people ship a blue box straight to your home. Inside that box is an array of Magic Bands, customized for each person traveling with you. These bands are similar to a Fitbit but without any of the demands on your heart rate. Each one has a tiny chip embedded to work as your room key, your ticket into the theme parks, and a dozen other uses on Disney properties. They are most aptly named; they are Magic, indeed. Once you get your Magic Band, the journey begins.

Also in that blue box you'll find your luggage tags for the airport, and here's what seals the deal: the tags have Mickey

Mouse on them. They basically shout that you're on your way to the happiest place on earth. Even the most distinguished professional, the premiere-level sales rep with a million air miles and a slick, silver travel suitcase will slap that bright red Mickey tag on her bag.

Disney makes every step of the journey part of the process. The excitement begins weeks before, and even the plane ride is exciting. Every detail becomes part of the experience, and the planning, packing, and shuttling to the airport are no longer just a means to an end. Disney knows how to make every moment count, even the boring ones. Instead of the normal queue lines, Disney creates an experience. They tell a story so sweeping that you hardly even realize you've been waiting for an hour. The long wait that normally feels useless has become a memorable part of the vacation experience. Those moments now carry meaning.

Hope in the Hard Moments

But not every day is a Disney vacation. In daily life, there is a real chance that things won't turn out like you thought they would.

Now comes the hard part, and this is where endurance matters: when the wait is longer than you thought it should be, the path is unclear, the road is harder, the destination is delayed—or you've actually gotten there, and it's not what you thought it would be.

How do you stay faithful in the messy middle?

How do you hold onto hope when you cannot see?

To hold onto hope, we must reject destination thinking and instead pay attention to what is happening within us along the way. Hope lies in this moment, not in the destination. Endurance becomes hope when we learn to stay in the moment we are in, to see what is happening here and now. That's how we make this moment matter, how we make everything part of the process.

We get a picture of this in Romans 8, one of the most precious passages in all of the Bible. The apostle Paul is writing to an audience compiled of some really good religious people and some really wild nonreligious people, all trying to follow Jesus together in a world gone mad. (Sound familiar?) The pressure of their culture is pressing in on them, and they seem to be losing their strength, their hope, and their endurance because things aren't turning out like they wanted.

These are the messy middles, where there's a real tendency to just escape and indulge in what the world has to offer. These are usually the moments when we make the worst decisions and continue the regret of our past.

Paul speaks right into this. He writes,

> "I consider that our present sufferings are
> not worth comparing with the glory that will
> be revealed in us." (Rom. 8:18)

He turns our attention to this space in between where we are and where we want to be, to pay attention to what is happening right now. Something incredibly important is happening, right in this difficult moment. He's saying, what you are experiencing is real, and there's a reason to call it suffering. But don't get discouraged by the progress that seems to elude you because something else is going on, a process you cannot yet see.

When moments get hard, our thoughts have the power to derail us into these sweeping realities of all or nothing. Regret sounds like, "I don't know how my life got this way." Fear sounds like, "I don't know how anything will ever get better." These two foes are magnetically drawn to each other, crushing your soul and stealing the life that is directly in front you. Paralysis takes over when the regrets of the past and the fear of the future continue to pile up like cars on the highway, blocking the path. We conclude that it will always be like this.

When we feel that time is wasting away, we need to stop, draw a point in time, gain perspective, and remind ourselves that who we are becoming is more important than what we do. You might read that and say, "But I'm not doing anything," and I say, "That doesn't mean something's not happening."

That's what you've got to see: so much could be happening in this process. Instead of "getting through" something, you have the power to assign meaning to the moments *you are in.* You can silence the fear and regret when you establish rhythms that move you toward who God has created you to be. Paul points us to that perspective when he compares our present condition with the hope that is available even while it's hard.

When your mind is racing day and night with the chaos that consumes you, you have the power to bring the train to a halt. The pattern of despair must be interrupted by naming the truth of the suffering you are experiencing. Remember what we learned from the prophet Jeremiah: to feel the emotions and name them. We need to consider this present condition, the pain that is happening in this moment right now.

And, like Jeremiah, Paul instructs us not to stay there. He points us to the good that is to come, God's faithfulness in this moment and in the process. The invitation is to consider that this present moment will give way to something that is yet to be fully seen. God is working in ways we cannot see.

We could allow all that overwhelms us to continue to pile up. But this is what threatens the moment. Don't lose hope in the messy middle. Drop a pin, mark where you are, create a conclusion, and find grace in this moment. ✻

CHAPTER 6

HOPE WHEN IT'S HARD

When You Can't See What's Next

THE SPRING OF 2020 introduced the world to the concept of social distancing. We all stayed home to flatten the curve of a pandemic that undermined every sense of normalcy in our everyday lives. Fear and anxiety were the emotions of the day as the headlines brought news of more illness, death, and community-wide lockdowns. Making decisions proved so difficult, and the criteria to make decisions got muddled into a medical, political soup. Information was everywhere, but the clarity seemed nowhere.

The hardest part wasn't sorting out the truth, though that proved impossible in the continued avalanche of information. The hardest thing was to make decisions in the midst of uncertainty. The future was not clear. With endlessly changing information and limited time to think, we had to make decisions that affected not only our own lives but the lives of others as well.

At some point the picture wasn't just blurry. It felt dark.

On March 12, 2020, my team and I made the difficult decision to suspend all of our public services at Port City Community Church. This was three Sundays before Easter. Ironically, the series we had planned for the month of March leading up to Easter weekend was titled "Hope in the Dark."

We had no idea how accurate that would be.

Preparation for Easter is insane during a *normal* year. It is typically the most attended weekend of the year, when everybody who hasn't been in church since Christmas makes their return. There are invitations—and sometimes bribery—from grandmas all over the land, who say this is the one thing they want: their family together in a row at church on Easter Sunday. Church attendance is off the charts.

That spike in attendance brings the added pressure to program service experiences that are engaging to those who are returning and to present the gospel in a fresh way to the occasional attendees. If people only come to church on Easter and if they always hear the same message they heard last year, they begin to wonder if there is anything else to the story. They start to roll their eyes and say, "Really, does this guy have any other tricks in his pocket?"

The inside joke is that Easter is the church's super bowl. We usually have six services, and it is all hands on deck. We start planning for Easter even before Christmas. I begin making notes and considering ideas and direction far in advance because I want to make sure my message is good.

Not because it's about me but because it is no fun to have to preach a bad message six times. I've done it before, and I'd like to never do it again.

A normal Easter brings a pressure of its own, but Easter 2020 was anything but normal.

Our entire experience had to be digital. The pressure multiplied itself many times over. Actually, the word *pressure* is an understatement for the vice we were in.

Easter is the time when we as a church remember the crucifixion of Jesus on Good Friday, and then we celebrate the resurrection on Sunday, but so often those two get squished in together like they're one thing. We pastors know they're inextricably connected but still different, and we want to honor them separately. But there are big decisions from a church planning standpoint: If we only get so much time with the people during Easter week, should we focus on the sacrifice of the cross? Or should we focus on the celebration of the resurrection?

As we were talking about Easter, talking together about hope in the dark, someone on our team quipped, "I wonder what Saturday would have been like for the disciples."

Talk about a messy middle.

When the Lights Go Out

Four Gospel writers wrote about the crucifixion of Jesus, and three of them—Matthew, Mark, and Luke—each make a point to mention that the world went dark when Jesus gave up his spirit. They each documented, "At noon, darkness fell across the whole land until three o'clock" (Matt. 27:45; Mark 15:33; Luke 23:44 NLT).

The light of the world literally went out.

Imagine that next day for the disciples and all of those closest to Jesus, to wake up after the exhaustion of the trials, the confusion of the Last Supper, and the horror of the crucifixion. I imagine they were exhausted and stricken with grief, but not just that. Everything they thought would be a certain way . . . it just wasn't. Everything they imagined—everything they hoped—is gone.

Sometimes we find ourselves stuck in the Saturday in between the crucifixion and the resurrection. Everything that we thought would be a certain way . . . just isn't. There is a lot to process in the messy middle, so much to mine out of the darkness. You're used to what you can see, hear, feel, and touch—used to using all of your senses to make decisions. But when the lights go out, all the senses we are accustomed to are no longer useful. We have to rely on something else.

When you can't see what is going to happen, you have to trust. This is what the Saturday feels like.

Darkness is the partial or total absence of light. It conceals things, and it prevents us from seeing. When the clarity we so desperately want becomes hidden from us, we become trapped in a mindset that repeats on a constant loop: "Get me out of here."

What do we do in those seasons? How do we move through the dark, even with the inability to see what is ahead?

Familiar Misery Beckons

As I write this, we are a world still in the throes of the pandemic. We want to see the end of this, and we desperately want to know when things will get back to normal. People are scheduling their vaccines, and social media is flooded with photos of first and second shots. Maybe as you're reading this, you know how it all ends, when it all ends. Right now we just don't know.

Our tendency is to work things out now, as quickly as possible. The harder we strain to see what is next, the greater the uncertainty we feel, and the more we want to get out from where we are. We tend to arrange our lives so that everything works together for our ease and comfort. When things get hard, we tend to think something is wrong. This creates the tension that keeps us from seeing what is happening in the moment. It is here that the pull to go back is so strong.

We desperately want to see those finish lines, but they are veiled, concealed in darkness. When darkness is disorienting and uncertain, we want to get back to what we had before—even if that wasn't a good or healthy situation. We may have actually been miserable before, but we feel safer returning to familiar misery than stepping into an unknown future.

When the Israelites came into the wilderness with Moses, they wanted to turn back to Egypt. Back in Egypt everything was easier. *Sure, we were slaves,* they thought. *But there was food!*

We read that and think how silly it was for them to long for a lifestyle of enslavement, but we do that, too. We are willing to give up our freedom if captivity feels more familiar. Familiar misery feels better than uncertain hope.

We love all the passages in the Bible that talk about God delivering us from things, getting us out of things. But a lot in the Scriptures is given to us about his meeting us in the middle of the hard things.

The tendency is to get out from under or to get around or to get over, but we actually have to go through them. The only way for us to embrace the process that is so important is to go through. And we go through one step at a time, as we depend on God to be gracious in this moment we are in.

In any season of darkness, our desire to "get back to normal" pulls us off track. If we cannot see what is coming next, we feel a distinct pressure that pulls us back to the familiarity of the past. But "back to normal" is not the direction God is headed. He's not going back to anything.

He is always doing something new.

If we rush back to what is familiar, we stand a strong chance of missing what God is doing in the present moment and the greatness he has in mind for the future.

Between the Invitation and the Promise

In the last chapter, we talked about how something is happening even when we cannot see it. Paul wrote a message of hope to the church in Rome. He said, "I consider that our present sufferings are not worth comparing with the glory that will be revealed in us" (Rom. 8:18). There's a promise right there, even in those first words: something is coming that is not fully revealed yet.

It feels painful and impossible to navigate when we are in the darkness, but there is an anchor in Paul's words, tucked between the invitation to consider our current condition and the promise that God is working all things together for good (Rom. 8:28).

There is an invitation to consider the difficulty, to embrace the moment. To feel what is happening without trying to minimize or pretend that this messy middle isn't overwhelming or threatening everything we hold dear. The promise that we rest on is this: something is coming that is not fully revealed. You're about to see something you cannot yet see, and that is the human condition.

So let's look at the messy middle from God's perspective, as recorded by Paul. You may have read or heard these words before, so I want to invite you to pay careful attention. Read this next section slowly and carefully. It packs a wallop.

> For the creation was subjected to frustration,
> not by its own choice, but by the will of the

one who subjected it, in hope that the creation itself will be liberated from its bondage to decay and brought into the freedom and the glory of the children of God.

We know that the whole of creation has been groaning as in the pains of childbirth right up to the present time. Not only so, but we ourselves, who have the firstfruits of the Spirit, groan inwardly as we wait eagerly for our adoption to sonship, the redemption of our bodies. For in this hope we were saved. But hope that is seen is no hope at all. Who hopes for what they already have? But if we hope for what we do not yet have, we wait for it patiently. (Rom. 8:20–25)

Deep breath. This passage is loaded.

There is a frustrated purpose and a groaning creation. What in the world is going on here? This is a great question.

There is so much to be understood here, as we think about this idea of forgoing the easy way, the temptation to escape, the choice to embrace the hard things in front of us. This is a promise. What we are going through right now, as hard as it is, is not worth comparing to this thing that will be done in us, this thing that will be made clear to us later on.

Look carefully at this line with me:

For the creation was subjected to frustration, not by its own choice, but by the will of the one who subjected it, in hope.

Let's consider this together. God created us, and God has called us to rule and to reign with him since the beginning of creation. We have been given the authority to exercise dominion as representatives of God himself, overseeing the world he has made. This is a pretty good gig.

The problem is that humans don't tolerate trust very well, and our decision to rule the world broke the world. Literally. Everything broke when those who were entrusted to care for the world failed to trust the One who created it.

If you think about the original creation, God has called us to rule and to reign, to exercise dominion, that the world would live in subjection to his rule given to us and through us. This is such a powerful purpose to consider. If you grew up in the Christian faith, you often heard that the gospel begins with bad news: human sin. You hear about depravity and original sin and the fall, which are important.

> HUMANS DON'T TOLERATE TRUST VERY WELL, AND OUR DECISION TO RULE THE WORLD BROKE THE WORLD.

But the epic beginning starts good—with a beautiful purpose and a glorious invitation.

We were created to create and contribute with God. With him. Together.

His intention was to allow us to live in communion with him, and out of that communion, we would continue to create and contribute to the culture of the world in the way God intended it to be—as an expression of his heart and his image, ruled by his love.

The Bible has a word to describe what the world is like when it's functioning like that: *shalom*. Shalom is an ancient word, often translated *peace*, but it is much more than our basic definition. Shalom is a way of life where everything is as it should be, rightly related to everything else. Shalom is the way of life where we are rightly related to God, and from that right relationship, we live rightly related to everything else.

Shalom got broken in the fall, and ever since then there has been this endless, grinding futility.

Peace seems just out of reach, and purpose eludes us. This is fertile soil for destination thinking to take root. Each time we try something and it doesn't work, we get frustrated. Our past fills with regret. Hope is deferred. The heart gets sick, and we get frustrated. Ever since then there has been futility. And that's a problem.

But God is up to something else. He doesn't offer an easy fix to our problem. Instead he brings the promise of redemption, the promise that he is at work to make things new. We actually know this more deeply than we think.

The Lion King

We make sense of deep concepts by stepping into a story, often one that may seem entirely unrelated. Our brains long to make sense of things we cannot understand, and we latch hungrily onto a story with a beginning, a middle, and an end. Sometimes the notes in the story strike a melody in tune with our soul, and we can understand what we've been longing to know. For this reason and with this intention, allow me to take a sidestep into a familiar story, one of the all-time great Disney classics, *The Lion King*.

The movie begins with a baby dedication of sorts, as Simba the lion cub, the son of Mufasa, is born into his royal destiny. Mufasa prepares Simba to be the next king of the jungle, but evil Uncle Scar wants to kill Simba so Scar can step into the role as the next king. Scar plots scheme after scheme to kill both the father and son, and while rescuing Simba from danger, Mufasa is killed in a stampede.

The pivotal event in the story is the moment we all dread. Simba discovers his father's body, and he tearfully pleads with Mufasa to wake up. Mufasa dies, and we stare at our screens. We all want things to go back to the way things were at Pride Rock. Bring Mufasa back.

Think about it. There is no tension or intrigue if Mufasa dies of natural causes and Simba naturally becomes king. Something has to happen to create the tension of the story. Something must make you think the world is over. The event that makes the story is the moment where the lights go out.

Things don't work out the way Simba or Mufasa hope. So Simba runs away. He figured there was no point so why bother. He believes his father's death is his fault, and futility settles over him. Futility is purposeless suffering, and it means the hardship of the circumstances that surround you have no meaning. They don't count for anything.

I think our hearts break for Simba here because we understand: why would we bother to stay if all is hopeless and nothing matters?

In the absence of finding purpose and meaning, we tend to take what we can get. We find the latest craze or buzz we can find along the way. Hakuna matata, right?

The world ruled apart from God is chock-full of opportunities to tantalize, indulge, and distract us from the futility that controls everything, and here Simba gets to the heart of the struggle. Our challenge isn't just the fact that we have created access to instant gratification but that instant gratification usually falls short of what is actually available, and perhaps of what God intended.

Simba starts a new life in the jungle with a warthog and a meerkat, all frolicking in the lagoon and eating bugs from under logs. He covers his sadness with something new, and he moves on as quickly and efficiently as he can. Simba has erased what has happened, he is enjoying the carefree life, but the distracted happiness is cut short when—WHAM! He collides with his purpose. He has an *encounter* that shakes him from his escape.

Simba isn't looking for Nala, but he finds her. He learns what had happened to his home, that the hyenas have devastated Pride Rock. Nala calls him to a new beginning, to return home to his rightful place.

Simba dramatically returns to his rightful place, and everything else finds its place once again.

We know this and we love this, not just because it's a great story line and exceptional animation. This is redemption. We love a redemption story.

But here is an often overlooked fact at the end of the movie: Mufasa is still dead.

The thing is, whenever people talk about *The Lion King*, they almost never talk about Mufasa dying. They tell the story of Simba finding his rightful place, and it comes as a result of the sacrifice of a king.

The redemption of the story is not when things go back to normal. In most stories they never will. Redemption comes in the making of something new.

The View of Redemption

In one of his letters, Paul reminds us that God is always working everything together for good. His promise is that he is making something new. We want this to happen today, right? Yes, because of our tendency to work everything for our ease, our comfort, and to solve our problems.

But redemption doesn't operate in the economy of solving problems. Redemption doesn't shy away from suffering or hardship, and it doesn't flinch in the dark. It isn't threatened when things shatter. Redemption is God's relentless pursuit to return everything to its intended place.

The promise of redemption doesn't prevent the lights from going out. In fact, it requires it.

The tragedy in *The Lion King* was not resolved, because the worst thing that could happen happened. And yet everything that happened would eventually play a crucial part of the story. No part of our story is ever wasted, and so that season of hardship you're experiencing—or even loss—is never beyond hope.

Hope is available in every moment, even when we feel hopeless, because we know God wastes nothing.

The Beauty of Broken Things

If something shatters, whether it's a character, a story line, a dream, or a piece of pottery, we might believe it is now useless. If I drop a vase, I might just sweep it up into a dustpan and throw it away. What else is there to do with it? We tend to expect that broken things are finished, done for, and we can't use them anymore. Brokenness is something to disguise, or else the brokenness is useless.

But there is an ancient art in Japan called *kintsugi*, a word that literally means "golden joinery" or "golden repair." An artist takes pottery that is broken and repairs it with gold.

The artist seals the joints, not to hide the brokenness but rather to use the brokenness. The brokenness becomes the beauty. Kintsugi has become both an artistic process and a philosophy; rather than breakage being something to disguise, the Japanese have embraced the break as part of the history and the purpose of the piece. The brokenness is not the end of the story, but it is a part of the story.

There's a reason we long for the end. It's because in the depths of who we are we long for things to be made right. But there is beauty in the brokenness, and it is not something to rush through or disguise. It doesn't need to be hidden, concealed, or managed, but rather it has the potential to become something beautiful. I believe that is actually God's heart for our broken world. He doesn't want to sweep it aside and be done with it. He wants to seal it and shape it into something even more beautiful. It is part of the story. ✷

CHAPTER 7

FINDING PERSPECTIVE

The Courage to Seek God's Way

MAYBE YOU HAVEN'T noticed this phenomenon in pop culture, but you guys: the Rubik's Cube is back.

Don't laugh when I say this, but when I see kids walking around with the colorful cube, twisting and turning to solve this iconic puzzle, I feel a surge of hope for the future of the world. This teaser from the eighties evokes a longing deep within me, this visionary hope that maybe we will return to the decade that gave us U2, Bon Jovi, and the mullet. (Come to think of it, mullets are back, too.) I can't deny the part of me that will always long for the vision for how things are supposed to be, how things were rightly related . . . back in the eighties. The eighties were truly the way things were supposed to be.

Funny how our longing for redemption is quickly replaced by a demand for the past. The old familiar has a way of hanging on, whether it is a good familiar or a not so good familiar. We live under this pile of memories that we have gotten used to. It feels good to remember them, and we want to go back.

Consider the Rubik's Cube, widely considered to be the world's top-selling puzzle game. The puzzle begins with all six faces showing one solid color, and then you twist and turn the pieces until the cube is a jumbled mix of colors scattered throughout each of the six sides. Your task is to restore the puzzle, spinning and rotating the sides until the colors come together again—first with two sides, and then layer by layer, until that last twist aligns all the colors where they belong. That's when you have to slam the cube down in victory. The puzzle is solved, and you are the master of difficult things.

We are solvers. We are conditioned to identify problems, to chase down the solution. We like the Rubik's Cube because it can be solved, but too often we apply a Rubik's approach to the problems of life. That's when the idea of redemption gets lost on us.

Once we identify a problem, we work to find a solution, twisting and turning and rotating, trying to figure out the right configuration and declare the problem solved. We keep manipulating the information and the circumstances. We demand for things to be the way they were before.

One more twist. One more turn. If we can just figure out the formula, everything will be like it should be. We can't stop until we do. We can almost see the solution, so we push harder, thinking we're almost there. From our vantage point it should work out. When it doesn't, we only become more determined about the way things should be.

That's how we get caught in a loop of continuing, how we keep ourselves from a life of conclusion. If we can't get the present to conform to the way it used to be, we just drag the past into the future, forever thinking we are one twist away from everything aligning.

Mullet Man

A few years ago, I took my teenage daughter and a couple of her friends to a music festival featuring rock-and-roll legends, Def Leppard and Journey. My childhood is pretty clear in my mind, perhaps slightly exaggerated in spots, but the big moments are solidly in place—including the soundtrack that was playing. No childhood is complete without these epic greats, and I wanted to educate my girls on the finer points of eighties glam rock and the accompanying fashions.

And that's when I spotted him in the audience: a man who was the absolute depiction of the 1980s, incarnate.

He wore an airbrush T-shirt with original artwork likely from Panama City Beach, and the entire sides of his shirt were cut out in giant ovals. Not just the sleeves but the actual sides of his shirt. He held both hands high in the "rock on" position, pumping to the beat. Boom-pop! Boom-boom-pop! This guy came to rock, and he did not disappoint.

Best part of all, his hair was an impressive mullet: all business in the front, and a long, flowing party in the back.

I'll admit, I was a little jealous. At least of the mullet.

But something was out of place. He was the perfect depiction of everything I remember about that decade, but this guy was in his late forties. As he had aged, he brought the eighties with him, all the way into a new millennium.

I mean, I get it. I may have mentioned that the eighties are one of my favorite decades, and there's something glorious about that season of big hair and metal bands. That's why I was at the concert, to be sure my daughter grasped the magnitude of the influence.

But the eighties ended a long time ago. And this guy wasn't willing to let go of those glory days. He'd likely never even considered the possibility of drawing it to a close, of leaving it behind. He had simply dragged his past into his future. The person he had been in the eighties was the person he was today. It had all just continued.

Are you clinging to past glories to define you because you can't imagine a different possibility?

When we don't draw our seasons to a conclusion, the glories of the past become the source of our hope. Like the mullet man who's still sporting his hairstyle, the retired cheerleader who is still talking about the time when she was homecoming queen, and the former quarterback who is still wearing his varsity jacket to his son's football games, we end up reliving and longing for the way things used to be—and the way we think things ought to be.

Other times we drag our shame along with us like a bad style. In fact, the longer you live with hard or bad things, wallowing in failure and disappointment, the more it starts to fit like a familiar sweater. You might even begin to believe that's what you deserve. There is comfort in familiar misery, and the loop will continue unless you do a hard stop. Whether you are sporting a mullet or wearing a scarlet letter, it doesn't need to define you anymore. Whether it was glorious or shameful, it is time to bring it to a conclusion. Your faded glory or haunting shame will steal God's promise for your future.

> WHEN WE DON'T DRAW OUR SEASONS TO A CONCLUSION, THE GLORIES OF THE PAST BECOME THE SOURCE OF OUR HOPE.

A hard stop involves a hard, honest look. Sometimes it calls for courage to step into the unknown. You may have to bring it to a conclusion, even if you can't yet figure out what is next. New things are created in the space where we draw conclusions. To find the new mercy for tomorrow, you have to be willing to conclude today.

Listen, if you have a mullet, keep it. But don't hold on to the past because you are afraid to let it go. The stakes are high, and your story is being written. Create space for something new to happen. As much as I still want a mullet and love the eighties (in fact, I am listening to Howard Jones right now), I don't live there anymore. New mercies aren't found there.

Solutions That Are in Our Hands

One of my favorite scenes in the Bible happens in the book of Joshua. Joshua is Moses' protégé, and they have a lot of similarities—though Joshua had some big shoes to fill. Both men knew the intimacy of the presence of God, both men led the Israelites, and both men led people across a body of water on dry ground when God parted the waters for two separate miracles. Moses is famous for leading the people across the Red Sea, and Joshua led the people across the Jordan River.

Same miracle, different outcome. Moses was leading the Hebrews out of bondage, and Joshua was bringing them into the promised land. Moses was leading them away from the problem, and Joshua was leading them into the promise.

In between the two, the Israelites spent forty years wandering, learning how to live as free people. (We will talk more about this later, so tuck it away in your mind for now.)

Joshua had been camping for three days with the Israelites preparing to cross the river. They had been wandering for forty years, and it was all about to come to an end—though they didn't yet know how. As Joshua was preparing to lead the people across the river, he gave them one instruction that was so important for crossing a threshold from what *was* into what *will be.*

> Joshua told the people, "Consecrate your-
> selves, for tomorrow the LORD will do amaz-
> ing things among you." (Josh. 3:5)

This verse does not say what we expect.

If you're about to head somewhere, and you're all geared up at the starting line, you expect the next words from your leader will be a charge to forge ahead. Like the starting words of every great beginning: Let's go.

But instead, Joshua does the opposite. Take a breath. Take a pause. Feel the conclusion.

To consecrate literally means to set apart or to declare as holy. It means to say, "This is intended for a specific purpose, and I'm going to make sure it is set apart for the purpose for which it is intended."

Note that this happened before they crossed the river, so it was an invitation to pause and consider the present moment, the conclusion of their season in the desert. Tomorrow, the *next* day, God was going to do something new.

I paraphrase Joshua's words this way: consecrate your-self today, for you have no idea what God is going to do tomorrow.

This was an invitation for the Israelites, but it's an invitation for us as well: to consider this present moment, whether it's been the worst season of your life or the best you can remember. Set yourself apart. Take a breath. Pause. Feel the conclusion. And give yourself some space so things can come to a close. Let your season be concluded, for God's about to do something new.

When the Waters Part

The next morning Joshua told the priests what God had said: "Lift up the Ark of the Covenant and lead the people across the river" (Josh. 3:6 NLT). The ark was a box made with precise detail and specific components, and it symbolized God's presence with his people. God said, "I want everyone to stand back as the priests walk by with the ark, and then I want them to walk into the river. When they get their feet wet, then the waters will begin to part."

Notice the order of operations: Feet get wet. *Then* the waters will part.

That's not how we prefer it, is it? We want to reverse it: part the waters, and *then* we'll go in. But God says no, I want you to get your feet wet, and *then* I'll part the waters.

A lot of people stand on the edge of the water, wondering why God won't do anything amazing to show them the way. And the reason is because we haven't yet done what he has asked us to do. He invites us to take a step, and when we follow him, he shows the next step. He's calling us to trust. Clarity does not come with knowing the path; it comes with taking the step.

He's always leading us to have faith—and then more faith.

Sure enough, the priests stepped into the water—a very high water, we should note. The description says, "The Jordan was overflowing its banks" (Josh. 3:15 NLT). The priests who were carrying the ark touched the water at the river's edge, and "the water . . . began backing up a great distance away," it says, "until the riverbed was dry" (Josh. 3:16 NLT).

The water opened up and the people crossed through safely while the priests stood on dry ground in the middle of the riverbed. And it's not a small group, let's remember. It's the *entire nation of* Israel, crossing the Jordan River on dry sand. We have an image in our minds that the people walked at a slow and easy pace, but I don't think that's how it happened. Imagine it. If you're walking through a river where the water has stacked up like a wall beside you, I don't think you're going to take your time on a leisurely stroll. You're going to hustle through there as fast as you can because you don't know how long this miracle is going to hold out.

They make it through, and I picture them catching their breath, maybe high-fiving one another and saying things like, "Did you see that? Can you even believe that just happened?" They have witnessed something amazing, and they can celebrate because it's behind them now.

Well, yes, but only partly true. God had done something amazing, but he was not ready for them to rush into the next phase of their journey. They needed to conclude this moment first.

God said to Joshua, "Choose twelve men, one from each tribe. Tell them, 'Take twelve stones from the very place where the priests are standing in the middle of the Jordan. Carry them out and pile them up at the place where you will camp tonight" (Josh. 4:2–3 NLT).

We cannot miss the drama of this situation. They've just made it across, but then God sends them back into the river—back into the *middle* of the river. They made it through maybe the scariest thing they've ever done, and then they had to go back. That would not be a normal choice.

Every time I read this story, I think of people I know who have braved their way through counseling. They make it through something difficult, and they want it to be over. But then the therapist says, "I think we should revisit this," inviting them back into the middle of high waters. It's not where they want to go, but it's the only way forward.

Joshua called together the twelve men he had chosen, and he relayed the instructions: "Go into the middle of the river. . . . Each of you must pick up one stone and carry it out on your shoulder" (4:5). So we're talking about some big boulders. Not little stones they can carry in their pocket but something so large that they need to leverage the strength of their shoulders.

He says, "Get twelve big rocks from the center of the river, and we will use them to build an altar." Why? So that, in the future, when your children ask you, "What are these rocks for?" you can tell them what God has done here on this day (Josh. 4:6–7, author's paraphrase).

There is an important distinction here, because Joshua is not leading them down a path of nostalgia. He's not trying to keep a Rubik's Cube around so the children of the Israelites can always remember how great things were, way back when, in what would mistakenly be called the four best decades of all time.

God was inviting His people to gather the stones and to build an altar as a reminder to be confident in what God has done in the past, for the sake of what he will do in the future.

Two Lists (Actually Three)

I learned to solve the Rubik's Cube after I bought a book called, *You Can Solve the Rubik's Cube in One Minute.* This was perfect: open the book, follow the steps. It spoke directly to the highest values in my quest: getting it solved, and getting it solved fast.

This might be your love language: solving problems fast. You are on a mission to do what needs to be done in the most efficient way. When we have a list of instructions, we feel a sense of control.

When I consider that story of Joshua and the Israelites, I imagine some people there questioned the efficiency of the whole thing. Why wouldn't God just part the waters and let the Israelites cross? Why make them start into the water before they know what will happen? This doesn't seem like the best way to get this done.

They built the stack of stones as a reminder of several truths: God is faithful, and we are invited to trust His faithfulness. He doesn't do things the way He has always done them, and He doesn't do things the way we would do them.

When you tell the story of wet feet and stacked stones, you don't start with walking in the river. You begin with the charge to consecrate yourselves. You begin with a conclusion. The season of wandering is over and the season of promise is beginning.

> God did not make us to follow instructions; he created us to walk with him. Clear instructions might be the most efficient way to execute your plans, but trust is the only way to experience a relationship.
>
> We tend to expect God to act in ways we can predict and understand. We default to this perspective quickly, especially when we cannot figure out how God is going to pull something off. We forgo the consecration and replace it with calculation. But God is not interested in getting us to where we want to go; he is inviting us to trust. The stones tell this story.

You see, most of us have two lists. We may not have them written down, but they exist, and they often reflect the way we relate to God.

List 1: Things I Would Like God to Do

This list is obvious, and it shows up in the ways we pray. Give me more money, a nicer car, better relationships, less annoying habits, and the list goes on. These are things you request of God, and your desperation will match your fervency in those prayers. (I am not suggesting we should withhold or censor our concerns before God, no matter how small they seem. We are in fact, instructed to pray about everything. I am just suggesting that an essential part of prayer isn't just request but gaining perspective in the presence of God.)

Now, the second list. This is a little more fun.

List 2: Things I Would Do if I Were God

I suspect you know what I am talking about. For example, if you had God's power and capacity, you probably know what would happen to the person who cut you off in traffic. You likely know who would be in the White House. If I were God, I would part traffic like the Red Sea. And there's no way I'd let anyone put a nail in my wrist.

(I have realized that it is a good thing I am not God.)

If we had God's power, we would make the world better by making our lives run smoothly. But Jesus did not come into the world to build a better world but to build his kingdom. This is a different way of operating. When we do not align ourselves to his will and his way, we end up attempting to use his power to solve our problems rather than pursue his purpose. We need to consecrate ourselves, to find a conclusion.

So we need a third list.

List 3: Things God Intends to Do

This list calls us to open our hands, to relinquish control, and to welcome the process. Remember, his promise is redemption, and this means God uses everything for the story he is telling. Redemption requires us to cling to the reality that God wastes nothing. So what does God intend to do? He will be faithful, and he will use every event of our lives to shape the story he is telling.

Don't project your will on his. You may have no idea how God is going to do what he intends to do, but that has no bearing on his capacity to get it done.

> YOU MAY HAVE NO IDEA HOW GOD IS GOING TO DO WHAT HE INTENDS TO DO, BUT THAT HAS NO BEARING ON HIS CAPACITY TO GET IT DONE.

God did not give us a set of instructions so we could follow them carefully, execute perfectly, and then slam the puzzle down in victory as the master of difficult things.

Instead of instructions to follow, he revealed himself and invites us to follow. He is the hope of our glory and the redemption of our shame. So we don't have to have a solution to trust his promise of redemption. We simply stop and offer ourselves, pieces and all.

Consecrate yourself. For he is doing something new. ✳

CHAPTER 8

THE PAST FINDS PURPOSE

When What's Finished Becomes Useful

JOE IS THE best neighbor you could wish for.

He knows who comes and goes in our neighborhood. He can hunt, fish, operate heavy machinery, bandage a wound, and captain a ship, along with a litany of other skills. He has about every tool you can imagine, and he will even let you borrow them. And usually when you borrow one of his tools, he comes along to use the tool he is letting you borrow. He brings his expertise to your need.

Joe also knows I am a pastor, which means I don't really have many usable skills, like sawing and hammering and fixing stuff. (I know lots of pastors who are good at things like that, but I was not bestowed these gifts.) My "home improvements" rarely end up improving anything. My pattern is, usually after three trips to Home Depot, I have to call someone to help me. I need help not only with the original improvement but now to fix all the things I broke in the process of trying to improve.

This is where the story picks up.

A few years ago, my wife and kids went out of town, and I decided at the last minute that I would remodel my daughters' bathroom. I had always wanted to try my hand at tiling a floor, and the kids' bathroom looked like a perfect opportunity to learn.

As I started measuring and thinking and planning, I noticed the floor was a little "soft" around the sink. A squishy floor is never ideal. I got down on my knees and pushed against the floor with my hands, and it felt like a thin sponge. Evidently, when the previous owner had repaired a water leak, he had not treated the damage to the wood. So I would learn to tile.

I started the work immediately—on a Thursday night at 8:00. I dove in, and it was actually fun to pull out the sink and the toilet and the flooring. If you've ever done demolition, then you know it can be invigorating. There is so much potential in taking on a new project, so many possibilities in the chance to start something new.

Plus, it can be fun to break stuff on purpose.

I tore up this and that. In record time, I'd taken out the sink, the toilet, the baseboards, and laminate floor. The bathroom was completely stripped down to the plywood, the rotten part completely exposed and ready for repair.

I texted my wife with a picture of the bathroom, and she texted me back, "Do you know how to put it back together?"

That was a good question. I needed a moment to think.

I had an idea, but more importantly, I also have the best possible neighbor.

Joe came over with lots of tools for me to borrow and him to use. We—and by *we* I mean *he*—began to remove the rotten part of the floor so we could replace it and remodel. He pulled out the saw and began to cut, and I assumed my role as an observer and occasional holder of things.

While I know that neighbor Joe is way handier than I am, I'm still aware that rotten plywood is not very sturdy. So, from my observatory, I offered him some advice: "Hey Joe, you might want to be careful, the wood's kind of soft."

Even as I write this, I can feel the belly laugh beginning to come. Joe, with his safety glasses on and his circular saw in hand, knelt down to begin cutting through the floor. As soon as he knelt, the floor gave way under his left knee, and my neighbor Joe fell like a tree—straight through the floor. In an explosion of sawdust and insulation, he landed in the crawl space down below. He was dirty and dusty, the saw blade was still spinning—these images are forever etched in my mind. He wasn't injured, but there was something else wrong. There was something new in the air . . . a smell. And a nasty smell, at that.

You see, when Joe fell through the floor, he landed on the plumbing trunk line, yanking out all the shower and

toilet drains on his way down. And we could tell right away—
or smell right away—that this flooring project had suddenly
become a plumbing project.

I had envisioned the fun of laying tile and making the
bathroom sparkle. I had not signed up for this. The thought
of having to deal with this deeper work haunted me. I
wanted to forget it.

Forget It

That kind of frustration isn't a stretch for most of us.
Many people live on the border of frustration. The trip there
is short.

Imagine you are frustrated because you can't fix something. Your car. Your house. Your marriage. Your kids. Your
bathroom. And you get to the end of your rope. You have
tried everything you can think of. And in your exhaustion,
imagine saying, "FORGET IT!"

What do these words mean?

In this context, *forget* doesn't mean "I won't remember it
anymore." That's impossible.

You mean you give up trying to reason and argue or twist
and turn. You have tried everything you can think of. You
can't see any way forward so you just "forget it." You give up.

It doesn't mean amnesia; it means *surrender*.

Let's read Isaiah 43 with this perspective of forgetting
as surrender.

Forget the former things; do not dwell on
the past. See, I am doing a new thing! Now
it springs up; do you not perceive it? I am
making a way in the wilderness and streams
in the wasteland. (vv. 18–19)

We like the call to a new season. But the new season
requires the end of the old. And the end begins with the
same exclamation you make when you can't fix what is
wrong: FORGET IT!

When you have done everything you can think of, perhaps it is time to think in a way you haven't yet thought.
This is the invitation. Do not dwell on the past. It is time to
release the grip your past holds and to no longer live under
its rule for your future.

Forget what you have always seen because you need a
new picture. God is doing something new. And you will not
see the new thing while you are focused on the old.

I love the picture and the lesson for us. When we finally
come to a rest, a conclusion—when the past is no longer
piling up and defining our future, we notice something
subtle: the stream isn't on the other side of the hard season
but right here, right now. The way is *in* the wilderness. The
stream is *in* the wasteland.

Then we get this real-life *Lion King* scene with hyenas
and birds of prey.

Let's read on:

> The wild animals honor me, the jackals and
> the owls, because I provide water in the wil-
> derness and streams in the wasteland. (v. 20)

These scavenger dogs and opportunistic birds honor God. How? Not in some kind of "Circle of Life" moment where they bow down but rather by simply drinking from the spring God provides right here, right now. A jackal isn't looking for a bucket to store water for later, nor is he going to look to the sky for the next rain cloud. He is drinking the water that has been provided.

The same can be true for us. We honor God by receiving what is offered in this moment and trusting him to be sufficient in the next. This allows us to forget our past—to surrender it—without discounting it.

Count or Discount

I had not bargained for the hassle of remodeling the bathroom. I had not counted on things being so difficult. As much as I wanted to snap my fingers and have it finished, I was going to have go through the process required. This isn't a big deal if we're talking about the renovation of a bathroom, but it becomes essential when we are talking about formation of your heart.

When we encounter difficulties, when things don't work like we want or work out like we hoped, we want to make the difficulty end as soon as possible, to snap our fingers. The desire to quit surfaces when our determination is met with more than we can bear. And in this something happens in our heart. Suffering and struggle have a way of undermining hope. There is almost nothing worse than getting your hopes up only to be let down again.

"Hope deferred makes a heart sick" (Prov. 13:12). This put-off hope has just allowed your past disappointment to anchor your soul in the sad reality that this is just the way things are. Nothing really matters. And so you continue, hope deferred.

When we get more than we bargained for, the way forward can feel futile. What's the point?

The point is that God is forming you and shaping you, and therefore, we do not need to be so quick to discount the hard things. We have been conditioned to think that if something is hard, then something is wrong. When something is hard, it just means it's hard. The world is broken, and it doesn't work like it should, so things can be hard, unbearably hard.

That place is where we need to stop. To reset and to be reminded. We can draw a conclusion, and when we are tempted to discount our frustration, we find a new way to count it.

Let's take a moment and look at how James (the half brother of Jesus) addresses a group of people who are facing enormous struggle.

> Count it all joy, my brothers, when you meet
> trials of various kinds, for you know that the
> testing of your faith produces steadfastness.
> And let steadfastness have its full effect, that
> you may be perfect and complete, lacking in
> nothing. (James 1:2–4 ESV)

James begins his letter by saying hello and then jumps right in saying the challenges you face matter. What you are going through carries significance, and it holds a beautiful purpose because you have a faithful God. So don't just put your head down and grind through it; count it joy.

Regard it as a gift; consider it packed with potential grace, the place where you will experience something more of God and his work in your life. And find him to be so unbelievably good and kind and faithful. This can be a jolting perspective, to stare into the hardship and determine it to be joy. But that is what happens when we encounter God; he awakens us to something more when we can't yet see anything else.

Once we can begin to see what God intends, James reorients to the things we already know.

We already know that a challenge makes us stronger. Resistance builds strength. So now we apply that to the crisis of faith we are experiencing. When we are about to give up and give in, the tenacity to trust will strengthen our faith in God's work and deepen our dependence on God's grace.

Then we allow this deepening dependence to affect us.

Take a breath right now. I want you to hear this next part.

This deepening isn't something you do but something you allow to be done in you. The promise is that you are being formed. The perseverance of your faith will have its full effect, leaving you perfect and complete. This isn't about being mistake free but rather being made full and whole. You have endured, and you have found that his grace is indeed sufficient.

But the full effect requires your full trust. You have to trust God in order to avail yourself and allow the season to find purpose within God's promise of redemption.

When I was remodeling the bathroom, I have to admit there were times in that process when I didn't know if we'd ever get to use that bathroom again. I thought we might have to lock the door, board it up, and reminisce together of the long-ago times when it had been ours to use. But we did finally finish, and we almost threw a housewarming party, inviting everybody to walk on the sturdy tile floor and flush the toilet, just for the satisfaction of knowing we could.

The bathroom was finished and ready to be used! Obvious, right?

It isn't as obvious as we think. Too often we hope to get over things or to get past things so we can get on with our lives. This tendency is driven by our desire to move on from them, putting them in distant memory. But just as my bathroom had to be finished before it was usable, so does your past. Finished things become usable things.

Do you want to experience God's promised redemption? Do you want to see how your past is a usable part of God's story for your future? Then it needs a finish.

The hard seasons do not become useful because we finally understand them, or because we ultimately endure them, or even because we resentfully get over them. When we become discouraged because we can't see how things fit, we can choose to trust that they are still essential parts of the story. Every event has its place in the story of God's grace and faithfulness in our lives. He is at work here, in this moment, and he began with the end in mind.

The promise is not that things turn out the way we want, only that nothing is ever wasted. This is why we don't have to run or shy away from the most difficult of experiences, nor do we have to be defined and confined by our successes. But rather, we can know that the testing of our faith will build strength. Our role is to "let perseverance finish its work so that you may be mature and complete, not lacking anything" (James 1:4).

Finished work requires finish lines.

Pick a Point—Draw a Line

I hate decorating for Christmas. I have decided this is a fact that is true about me. I'm a husband, a father, a surfer, and I do not like decorating for Christmas. Not at all. Hatred might be an appropriate word, and when I do it with a good attitude, it's evidence that God is doing a good work in my heart. This is evidence of his presence in my life, I assure you.

We have a tree that we've been setting up for more than twenty years. Every year, we bring it out of the attic, and we set it up again. People ask, "Do you have a fake tree?" No, I have a real tree. It's artificial, but it is real. It is not imaginary. It is a real, artificial tree.

I wish I could show you the box that holds our Christmas tree. It's beat up, damaged, and wrapped in duct tape. I think it is actually the duct tape that holds it together. Rather than ever getting a new box, I just keep taping this one together, year after year. Every year I cut it open, take the tree out, put it up, wrestle with it, and let it live in my house for the season. Then I take it back down, I put it in the box, and I put some tape around the box to close it up again. As I write this book, there are now twenty-four layers of duct tape on this box.

I used to gripe about it. Now I have this kind of ritual. This tree is usually the last thing I take down. I stand and look at the tree; the lights and ornaments are removed, and it now stands in its undecorated state. I pull the box out and carefully fold the flaps back. Duct tape ribbons roll off and stick to everything. There is the standard gray. But then there is an array of colors. Each stripe of tape marks the close of a season. I stop and look at all the lines. Each line carries with it a season that has become a part of our story; it has become a part of this moment.

Some of those years were so hard I wasn't sure how we'd make it. Other years were so full I didn't want them to end. But whether it was good or bad, full or just full of stress, each one got a stripe of duct tape. And each one mattered to what has become of us.

And so after twenty-four years, there's a little pause, call it a conclusion. The memories are sweet, and part of me longs to return. But a beautiful hope pulls me ahead. And so, in that moment, I pack the tree into the box and grab the duct tape and begin strapping it shut. It is finished, and it is packed away, usable for the next season.

The same is true for that ongoing thing from your past that needs to find a conclusion: it is finished. And now it becomes usable. The season is now absorbed into the story.

You may need to take a strip of tape, a stripe of color, pick a point, and draw a line. You don't declare it finished to declare it over but rather to trust that it mattered. Finished things are usable things. ✳

PART THREE

ENDURANCE
BECOMES HOPE

—————————————————

Hope is found with grace *for* the moment. This section helps us understand the sufficiency of God's grace and the security of his promise of redemption.

CHAPTER 9

SCARS AND STORIES

Finding God's Faithfulness

I HAVE A scar on my back. It's not super noticeable, not like something so distracting that it would make you call me Scarback. But if you look closely, you'll see a small spot, about a half-inch long, that is slightly raised and whiter than the rest of my skin. No stitches were required, but it bled like I was going to need a transfusion. Like every scar, it has a story.

The story of the scar happened at a water park when I was in high school. Do you remember water parks and waterslides, the whole routine? You would stand in line, get ready, and take your place on the slide. The lifeguard would say something like, "Sit down, cross your ankles, cross your arms, and go on my call." He would wait until the slider in front of you had rounded the bend and started full speed down the flume, and then he'd give you the signal to go.

For some reason, we thought it was cool to create a human pile on the long curvy waterslide. One of us would be the designated piler, and we would stop just after that bend where the lifeguard was watching. He'd let the person behind you go, and then people would pile up, one after another, and then we would all end up together when we splashed down at the end.

But you aren't allowed to start out together because the lifeguard at the top of the slide makes everybody go one at a time. Those lifeguards were onto our shenanigans, and they were trying to prevent the human pile we were about to create. But we persisted.

I was the first one, and my job was to start the pile. With my ankles and arms crossed, the lifeguard said, "GO!" And off I went. I crossed the designated line, and then I positioned my feet and hands on the dry part of the waterslide to slow myself down to a complete stop. And then I waited. Someone would come after me, slow his roll down the slide, and add to my pile up.

The only problem is that Alan was behind me. Alan was excited. Alan was so excited that he forgot to go slow. When Alan rounded the bend, he was going way too fast to stop. I saw him coming, and I tried to prop myself up by my hands and feet, arching my back so he could go underneath me.

My plan almost worked, except for how excited Alan was. As he came zipping around the corner, he was laughing. Hard.

Now is a good time for me to tell you: Alan had braces on his teeth.

As Alan went under me, he almost cleared me . . . except that his braces caught on my back. Yep. Exactly like you think, exactly what you're picturing. As I said, I bled like I needed a transfusion. All the way down the slide.

So now there is a scar and a story because the two usually go together. We usually only appreciate the story after the fact, though. In the middle the story feels like survival.

Visible scars have a way of leaving invisible scars as well. The scar carries a sense of fear, a memory of pain, a reminder of what to avoid, and a promise never to let it happen again. We think our past gets buried under those scars, but without closure it is dragged into our future. It just starts piling up. Like Alan coming in hot, our past just comes barreling around the corner with too much momentum to stop on its own.

We can try to go faster to outrun it, or we can try to get out of the way, getting nicked again and again. Sometimes when the misery never seems to end, we have to force a conclusion. This isn't to avoid or to escape but rather to see the story clearly.

Separate to Create

In sports, when a coach calls a time-out, he or she is creating a disruption. If your team is losing, you can call a time-out to give your team a minute to break the pattern and interrupt momentum.

In music, a rest brings a literal pause in the sound. The beat keeps the sound from being static, and it provides rhythm to the melody.

In a five-course meal, the chef serves a palate cleanser to separate the complex flavors and to remove any lingering aftertastes from the previous course. You can't enjoy your cheesecake if you're still tasting your lasagna.

All of these are examples of intentional disruptions, of creating a separation of one thing from another.

Did you know that separation is an act of creating? The story of creation—the epic beginning we looked at—is a beautiful picture of creating by separating. The process is defined by dividing lines, where one thing stops and another thing starts. The dark ends where the light begins. Waters above are separated from the waters below. The land divides the oceans. These lines create space and establish something new.

As I write this book, my one word for the year is *detail*. I love details. I'm an architect by trade, and I love to look closely at creations, to notice the detail with which they have been made. Detail invites you to look more closely, to gaze more intently, and to experience something more fully. This is how we want to experience hope, with an eye for detail.

I chose *detail* as my one word for this year because I want to see the details of God's mercy, to learn what it means to walk with him in intimacy, in the intricacy of what he has made our relationship to be.

Many things inspired me to choose this word, but one unlikely source came from the book of Leviticus.

Leviticus is the third book in the Bible, and it's a strange one. It is the graveyard of the Bible reading plan. After a few days of dry reading about animal sacrifices, the lobe of the liver, split hooves, and chewed cud, most people abandon their pursuit to read the Bible in a year.

(I need to confess that I was reading Leviticus to prepare for a series that centered on sacrifice. I don't want you to think I was reading it for fun.)

In this peculiar book, the repetition and the specificity intrigued me. Call it detail. When the people sinned, they had to remove themselves from the assembly and quarantine. (Anyone? Too soon?) After a time away, they could come back, take a bath, and then they'd be clean again. We learn that cleanliness was connected to time.

Bad case of acne? You've got to wait a week before you can come back.

A mole with a white hair? You're out for a few days.

Caught touching a creepy crawly bug? You've got to stand in the corner.

Someone slices your back open with the braces on their teeth? I've always wondered how much time that would require.

Time was used as a detergent to cleanse personal unholiness and maintain corporate holiness.

Leviticus is filled with rules and consequences, each one like a holy time-out. This seems so foreign (and boring) to read, but the truth is, we use a similar tactic in our battle against sin—or at least in our attempts to prove our sorrow and our desire to change.

Remember the pressure of the streaks? This is the kind of scorekeeping I'm talking about. Maybe you struggle with something you wish you could conquer. Cussing. Pornography. Anger. Alcohol. Yelling at the kids. We all have something. When we do it, we feel so terrible, and we say we'll never do it again. We might even punish ourselves to atone for our sin and try to create a new pattern by keeping track of the time that separates us from what we did wrong. We feel better about ourselves as time passes.

"I haven't lost my temper in twelve hours."

"I haven't cussed in twelve days."

"I haven't had a drink in a month."

We count the days, and we think our past gets redeemed through the passing of time. But what we are actually doing is hoping that the further we get from our failure or our disappointment, the less our soul or memory holds the regret of it. We're trying to separate ourselves from the shame. We try to outrun or outlast our past. Yet it piles up with patterns that build history, momentum, and pressure. Even if we can get it out of our heads, we can't get it out of our hearts. We tell ourselves the darkness is behind us, that only good days are ahead. We try to convince ourselves that the old has gone, the new has come, when nothing has changed but the date.

We cannot convince ourselves that the old has gone. We have to reorient to a new way.

And this brings me to another critical thing to understand: Leviticus sits between the exodus from Egypt and the entrance into the promised land. This is important in the story of God's people. Leviticus—with all of its details and rules and blood and gore—marked a separation from the yoke of slavery, creating a new life of freedom.

God was saying, "You're not slaves anymore. You're my people. We're doing this differently." Leviticus shows us how critical it is to end a season and how difficult it is to reorient to a new way. All sorts of things work against us.

Leviticus also details a system that required the people to bring an animal sacrifice to restore their broken relationship with God and atone for their sins.

You can think of atonement as "at-one-ment"—the people could once again be rightly related to God. Atonement means I am forgiven, and therefore I'm all right with God, and God's all right with me.

With that in mind, let's read what Leviticus says about the animal sacrifice: "For the life of a creature is in the blood, and I have given it to you to make atonement for yourselves on the altar" (Lev. 17:11).

Slow down and see those words.

For *you* to make atonement for *yourselves*.

You might read that and think, "I don't see the problem." And that is the problem.

You've lived your whole life trying to do enough to make atonement for yourself—to make yourself right with God and to make God all right with you.

And how's that working?

We try to follow the rules. We try to keep it all straight. We try to separate ourselves from the sin that defines us by keeping time. And we continue to ask God, Am I good enough? Am I holy enough? Am I perfect enough? Our surrender starts over again every Sunday, and we always promise to try harder and to do more. But it does not work this way.

When we cannot atone for ourselves, we cannot find separation from our sin, and we cannot find closure. Only God can do that, and he did. More on that to come.

We have already read what King Solomon wrote: "Better is the end of a thing than its beginning" (Eccl. 7:8 ESV). The end trumps the beginning because everything that happens in between matters. It is becoming a part of God's redemptive story. Remember, nothing is ever wasted.

The proverb continues with another contrast, so let's read the entire verse.

"The end of a thing is better than its beginning; the patient in spirit is better than the proud in spirit" (Eccl. 7:8 NKJV).

Oftentimes we will read something in our Bibles that resonates and underline it. Better is the end—that is cool. The whole verse gets underlined because it resonated, not because we understand. We've looked at the tension of beginnings and endings, but how is this connected to pride and patience?

Pride is other people, right? Not us.

Pride is sneaky and hard to recognize. Especially when we are enduring a hard season. But pride isn't always about brash behavior or bragging about your accomplishment. Pride can manifest as a subtle resistance to endure, a defiance about what you have to put up with. Pride can send us in to a spiral of thoughts: if I did better, I wouldn't be here. If I didn't do that, then this wouldn't have happened. The haunting question of *why* leaves us second-guessing and overthinking. We are either the determined hero who will tough this out or the doomed victim who will remind everyone of how we've been wronged.

Pride makes us believe we don't need help or shouldn't have to put up with this.

Patience, however, is required to remain and not rush ahead. And patience is required for acceptance and healing.

There is a whole thing that happens in the space between a finish and a start. Finding a conclusion can serve to break momentum, create a rhythm, or get rid of the aftertaste of what you've just experienced.

These intentional points provide perspective and reorient us to the way of life we've been created for. At least that is my prayer, that you would stop and bring everything else to a stop with you.

Don't run from or run past these moments because it is in these very places that we feel. We feel the pain or regret or shame. We've managed to avoid these by continuing to move, always forging ahead. But healing doesn't happen on the run. A scar marks the closure of a wound, and as long as the wound remains open, there is no scar. If there is no scar, the story is unfinished.

IF THERE IS NO SCAR, THE STORY IS UNFINISHED.

We need a rest and a reset. We need to be reoriented to a new way.

Reoriented to His Way

A reset is actually written into the law of Leviticus. It is a beautiful idea, a foreshadowing to a restoration, a redemption, and a return—a return to the way things are intended, not to the life you knew before you were hurt.

The whole system was arranged around the calendar—the festivals, the Passover, the feasts, and the Sabbath. Every seven years was also a Sabbath year, when the land would lie fallow to recover and rest from its productivity.

We have to remember, they didn't have watches and iPhones to keep track of time. Think about this. Have you ever lost track of what day it is? It happens to me all the time. Heck, I've even forgotten what year it is. And when I do, I only have to look at my phone, and it immediately reminds me of my relation to the time-space continuum.

Their whole system of law established ways to pay attention and track time, which required incredible attention to detail. Watchmen were positioned to watch for the moon to appear and mark the beginning of the month. Every sunset marked a day, and every seven sunsets reminded God's people to trust—to rest. The system was designed to help us live in relationship to the Creator and the creation with which we have been entrusted. ✳

CHAPTER 10

THE POWER OF DISRUPTION

Turning Declarations into Questions

SUMMER IS MY favorite time of the year.

I love the heat.

I love the humidity.

I love the freedom.

I love the songs—"School's Out for Summer," "Summer of '69," and "Summertime." (I could go on, but a book is only allowed so many words.)

Buddy the Elf said smiling is his favorite. Summer is my favorite.

Believe it or not, not everybody loves summer. I know it's hard to understand, but I know people who actually prefer the cold. But even those extremists eventually get so sick of shoveling snow and arctic windchill that they, too, long for the tropics. It's possible to long for summer simply because you're sick of winter.

This is important.

It is possible for us to want something not because we like it but because we don't want to be where we are anymore.

(I'd underline that sentence.)

But as much as I have loved summer all of my life, at one point I began to feel a sort of low-level frustration that took me a while to identify. I couldn't figure out why I was irritated during the season I loved so much. It still had all the same elements I loved: heat, humidity, long days, no homework.

Hold on. It's that last one that pointed to my frustration.

Every summer, the kids would be home . . . with nothing to do. Days and weeks stretched before us, all without structure, routines, and predictability. We had waited and waited for summer, and suddenly we're on a countdown to fall. Not because we longed for the fall but so that things would go back to the way they were—the way they're supposed to be.

DISRUPTIONS REVEAL THINGS ABOUT US THAT PREDICTABLE PATTERNS AND CONTROL TEND TO MASK. THERE IS POWER IN DISRUPTION.

We thrive on rhythms and routines. Mostly, we love to control our schedule, and summer disrupts that. Disruptions reveal things about us that predictable patterns and control tend to mask. There is power in disruption.

During the school year, everything in my schedule—and everything in my world—works like it's supposed to. My wife worked as an administrator in the school my kids attended.

This worked out great for our family for many reasons. One of the advantages is that it created a helpful rhythm.

I remember the patterns well. After-dinner routines were often centered around preparing for the next day. Packing lunches, homework checks (or sometimes I'd be doing homework), getting the coffee ready to brew (because that could derail everything).

My wife and I would wake up early, I'd bring her coffee in bed, and we would ease into the morning together. We'd get up and start all "the getting"—getting ready, getting breakfast, and getting the kids moving. Five days a week. I'd get backpacks and lunches organized, and I'd get everybody in the car by 7:23, and then I'd get to wave as they backed out of the driveway.

And at 7:30 I had my morning. Amid the chaos of raising two daughters and leading a fast-paced church, my mornings became important. These were often spent at the coffee shop, sitting on the beach, or by the pool. This was the time when I tended to my own walk with Jesus, praying and reading and writing.

I guarded this time fiercely. Five days a week for nine months. I developed a rhythm. Enter my favorite time of the year. Instead of the familiar joy and anticipation, everything felt like it had gone off the rails. And when something messes with your well-established, effective rhythm—well, let's just say it doesn't go well.

I realized this on vacation, when I was frustrated *on vacation*.

It took a little soul searching for me to figure out that my mornings had been hijacked. All the disciplines I'd carefully orchestrated for those nine months—journaling, Bible study, morning coffee—were completely out of whack. Suddenly I was cooking breakfast for everybody. Everything was messed up. Everything.

And this idea of disruption brings me right back to the all-or-nothing perspective that can pile up and leave us paralyzed.

Understand the Seasons

Change is disruptive. Even the change we want.

But most of us don't respond as well as we'd like to think we do to the change that comes. I used to think only older people got stuck in their ways, but I learned that it happens to everyone, and it happens faster than we think.

It doesn't take long for rhythms to become familiar routines.

When I was a youth pastor, I remember the summer when I needed to choose a new destination for our summer camp. For two years the camp had been up the road in a cabin setting out on a river. The location was expensive, and it couldn't accommodate our growing number of students, so it was time to choose a new place. We moved the location to a convention center on the beach.

You would have thought we'd changed the Bible.

The kids protested with indignation, "We've never done it like this before!"

Wait a minute. You've been to that camp exactly two times, and it's a nonnegotiable? Two years of one location, and you can't consider something different? They resisted the idea that anything could compare to what they knew.

And that's when I realized: even for teenagers, it doesn't take long for patterns to become familiar and for nostalgia to sink in.

(It occurs to me that this is perhaps why I love the eighties so much, but my kind of nostalgia makes sense. The eighties were awesome, and nobody can convince me otherwise.)

When we get nostalgic, we tend to think everything was better back then. It's where we get terms like "the good old days." We tell ourselves that everything was fine back then. It wasn't fine, just familiar.

The fear of change, even subtle resistance to change, makes us long for the way things used to be. And we forget it was just as crazy then, with its own set of challenges.

Everything is always changing. The thrill of things being different means that something familiar is ending. As we confront the end of something, we encounter a conclusion. And we hit the brakes. No thanks, we say. I'd rather not.

We resist the necessary disruption that change requires. When everything seems to be changing, resistance becomes most fierce. We often search for ways to justify or defend the way things were, and we remain stuck in dead-end jobs, toxic relationships, and unhealthy patterns. The uncertainty that is inherent in change produces a real fear of the future.

When we feel the shaky ground of uncertainty, our instinct is to look for solutions, to find answers. We search for the relief of certainty in the face of uncertain chaos.

Don't get me wrong—it's important to get answers. But it's far more important to ask the right questions. Right answers to the wrong questions will draw you right back to the way things have always been.

The courage to conclude is often found in your willingness to ask new questions.

The right questions are better than the right answers to the wrong questions.

Declarations and Questions

I'm a pretty laid-back guy, though I am fairly intense. Instead of being rattled by stress or pressure or pace, I tend to feed on it. In retrospect, I have come to learn that this is perhaps more a function of naivete and just being unaware of the pressure or stress I should have felt, but—either way—it's equally effective.

I remember the first time the idea of vision, growth, and possibility paralyzed me. Port City had grown exponentially, multiplying itself from a church plant into numbers that qualified as a megachurch. We had a giant building, thirty-two acres, and thousands of people attending each weekend.

Like I said, per my tendency, I had been fairly naïve to what was going on as we were growing. I didn't realize how big things had gotten.

One year I attended an annual conference for pastors, but this time I was surprised with an invitation to participate in a breakout session for leaders deemed "effective." Evidently I had made the list. I remember looking around the room and seeing authors of books I had studied, thought leaders who had affected my thinking, and culture shapers I had learned from—albeit from afar.

Now I was invited to talk with them, meet with them, belong with them. And it felt strange. I felt like I was sitting in somebody else's seat.

When I returned to the office after the conference, instead of taking my same route to the usual parking spot, I took a long tour around the church. I circled the property in a wide loop, taking it all in.

And that is the first time I understood the meaning of the words *panic attack*.

My heart raced. My chest felt tight. My breaths were short.

I gripped the steering wheel, and I said, *I don't belong here. I don't know what to do. What have I done?*

This wasn't meant as a question. It was an expression of frustration disguised as a question.

I was in over my head. I was overwhelmed, truly wondering what I had done. What had I gotten myself into?

I wanted out.

I mean, I didn't really want out. But I wanted the option to get out.

(That might be when I first began to think through my escape plan, which is a pipe dream I have of making hammocks in Saint John. Paul was a tentmaker, so why can't I be a hammock maker? Yes, he made tents to support his ministry, and I'd be making hammocks to escape mine. But please, just let me have this dream. If I ever disappear, look for me in Saint John. Show up, say hi, and I'll give you a great deal on a hammock.)

We can be overwhelmed by either failure or success. Either way, the fear of the uncertainty makes you want to run away. Our tendency to run leads us to likely repeat what we've already done, to drag out our familiar past. We try to repeat the familiar successes, holding onto some former glory, fearful that it won't be available in our future. We decide to do what we've always done rather than to rely on the grace that is pulling us forward. Grace is always more effective than familiarity, though it feels uncertain.

When we are overwhelmed by what lies ahead, we make vast declarations, disguised as questions, that can paralyze us. For example, "What have I done?" is actually a declaration that I don't belong, and it is a statement that I don't know what to do.

We don't need to make declarations.

We need to ask questions.

We need the *courage* to ask the right questions.

A lot of times those questions are already there, but they are hidden by our frustration. We need to peel back the frustration and turn the statement into a question.

Remember in Isaiah 43, God is talking through his prophet Isaiah about a new thing:

> Forget the former things; do not dwell on the past. See, I am doing a new thing! Now it springs up; do you not perceive it? I am making a way in the wilderness and streams in the wasteland. The wild animals honor me, the jackals and the owls, because I provide water in the wilderness and streams in the wasteland, to give drink to my people, my chosen, the people I formed for myself that they may proclaim my praise. (vv. 18–21)

In my nature of paraphrasing, I see that God is basically saying through Isaiah, "I'm doing something new, and it includes you. I'm going to cause you to become the thing I intend you to be. It's a new thing. It's ahead, it's forward, it is something that hasn't yet happened to you."

And then he asks us a question, "Don't you see it?"

And we shake our heads. No, we don't see it.

This is where we stay stuck. We cannot see what is ahead, we cannot tolerate the disruption, and we keep doing what we've always done. We reach back to what has been because it was fine. It wasn't fine; it was just familiar.

God is saying, "You don't know because you haven't asked."

Look at the next verse with me:

> Yet you have not called on me, Jacob." [This
> is a name for Israel, the people of God.] You
> have not wearied yourselves for me, Israel.
> (Isa. 43:22)

Basically, he says, "I am doing a new thing, and on top of you not seeing it, you're not even asking me about it. You just keep looking around you for answers, but you're not asking the right questions. When you're ready to know the new thing I'm doing, you can start by asking me. I'll be happy to tell you."

So, when I reframed the statement, "What have I done?" to a question, I begin to recognize that I have tried to walk with God and to be faithful to him in what he has asked me to do. The pressure I feel to have all the answers begins to give way to the reality that I only have to stay close and stay faithful to him for what is to come. This leads to questions I can actually begin to consider.

> What do I need to do next?
>
> What do I need to learn?
>
> What is my next step?

When I allowed these questions to frame my next steps and establish the next season, then I could begin to see things I had never seen before.

The Courage to Ask

I have this theory, that when a man turns thirty-two, he has locked into the haircut he'll have for the rest of his life. The only reason I don't have the same spiky haircut of my twenties is because I'm a girl dad, and my daughters are not afraid to make me uncomfortable for the sake of keeping a relevant haircut. Otherwise, I'd still have the same spiky hair.

It's one thing when it's your hairstyle, but sometimes habits go far deeper. We master what we've learned, and then we execute what we've learned. Then, because it works, we stop learning new things. When we hold too tightly to things, we will never learn how to let go in order to get to something new.

We also do this with our suffering and struggles. If we have overidentified as victims, everything serves to protect our position of being wronged or hurt or harmed. If we overidentify with our successes, then we confuse our success with our identity and worth.

If someone asked, "Who are you?" what would you tell about yourself first?

What's the first thing that comes to mind?

What is your core identity? What are the things you hold on to?

Or, maybe better said, what are the things you won't let go?

This is where a disruption is important, even if it is uncomfortable. A disruption gives you the space to find the courage to ask God what he might be doing, rather than repeating what we've always done.

Disrupted Expectations

Let me ask you a couple of questions.

First: *Do you believe that life will work out exactly as you have planned for it to work out?*

Of course not. Everyone knows this.

Second question: *Do you live as though your life will work out exactly as you have planned for it to work out?*

Probably you do. We all do.

We spend so much energy on being frustrated when our carefully made plans are interrupted and our expectations are disrupted, even by the disruptions we expected.

Our lives are full of things that didn't go the way we wanted them to go. The disappointment can nag at our hope for the future. But the present is available. Right here, right now.

We have to wage war against regret. We have to disrupt the magnetism of old patterns. And we do this by being faithful in the moment, when we declare the past will no longer prevent the future by continuing to pile up. Faithfulness in the moment requires us to bring that season to a conclusion, to seize the moment underneath our feet and be faithful in it.

It is a thought so freeing that it bears repeating: we break the patterns of the past by choosing to be faithful in this moment. That is the only thing required of us.

New Answers Come from New Questions

In the book of Luke, the people ask Jesus a question about fasting, "Hey, Jesus, why do your disciples not fast when the disciples of John and the disciples of the Pharisees fast? What's the deal?" Jesus answers, "Well, while the bridegroom is here, you party, right? When the wedding is in full swing, you feast. When the wedding feast is over, you fast."

Then he told a parable: No one tears a piece from a new garment and puts it on an old garment. If he does, he will tear the new, and the piece from the new garment will not match the old (see Luke 5:36).

We can relate to this, right? You got a new pair of jeans and an old pair of jeans. You don't tear up the new pair of jeans to make a patch for the old ones. You just use the new ones. And Jesus goes on with another example: no one pours old wine into new wineskins. Otherwise, the new wine will burst the skins, destroying the skins and spilling the new wine. The new wine must be put into new wineskins.

The picture is that these two things are incompatible, and Jesus seems to indicate the new is better. If you try to mix and match them, it's going ruin both. He says you can't embrace the new and the old.

Then he says this in the next verse, "And no one after drinking old wine wants the new, for they say, 'The old is better'" (v. 39).

Look at what he says—if you keep drinking what you've always been drinking, you never know anything new. You'll think the old is just fine. If you keep doing what you've always done, you'll never want to do anything new because you'll believe what you're doing is fine.

Let's apply this to our understanding of God's work.

The old way of thinking is what Dallas Willard called "the gospel of sin management."[5] This looks like, "God, can you help me tame my vice? I drink too much, I smoke too much, I cuss too much, I'm mean. Can you help me get rid of this thing? Can you help me stop doing the thing I don't want to do?"

Which can lead to, "Don't do anything crazy. Just change me enough so I can get along with my life."

But God is not interested in just changing what you do. He wants something new. To change who you are. He wants to form you into the image in which he has created you. He empowers you to live out his created intention in each moment, in every season.

As in Isaiah, God said, I'm doing a new thing—don't you see it? And we don't because we haven't asked. Sometimes we need to stop and ask a new question. This will most likely create disequilibrium but will reveal things we need to see. When we encounter a new perspective, we start to ask new questions.

If you're feeling stuck or frustrated, it could be because you're asking the same question over and over. Guess what happens when you ask the same questions over and over? You get the same answers.

We have to start asking some different questions about who we are and what God is doing. We need to spend some time asking, seeking, knocking, looking to try to understand what God is doing.

But we are not going to get to the future unless we learn to let go of the past. We have to create a disruption that will force us to think differently, to consider things from a different perspective.

I am asking you to prepare yourself for the new thing God is doing. If we are not intentional to prepare ourselves, then we will fall back into the old patterns, and we will do the same things all over again.

New ways require new patterns, and new patterns require the old ones to be disrupted. This is how disequilibrium and disruption cultivate endurance.

Physical endurance requires a lot of disequilibrium. A lot of pain at times. Our legs ache, our muscles are sore, our lungs burn as we push through things in order to get stronger and build endurance for what is to come. Suffering produces endurance in the physical sense, and it also does so in the spiritual sense.

Endurance produces character. It creates substance for our identity. It gives weight to who we are.

And character produces hope (Rom. 5:3–5).

This is the process in which hope happens.

We rejoice. We give weight to our suffering. We enter into the hard places because suffering produces endurance. Endurance is simply the refusal to stop short. We refuse to stop believing when we cannot see. Hope is what keeps us from stopping short. Hope keeps us in the game. We demonstrate hope when we continue in faith.

All of this requires a foundation that is sufficient to bear the weight of what we're going through. We've been given that foundation in Christ. We have to trade in our dependence on control and certainty. And we have to learn to place our trust in him.

The beautiful thing about the gospel is this: when we couldn't see a way—how in the world could the end of Jesus' life actually be the most beautiful thing for us?—God was still working. We didn't know. But Jesus was making a way. In fact, he said, *"I am the way."*

Every day that you wake up and decide not to give up and decide to continue to walk in faith, knowing God is in charge, you are demonstrating hope. Even when you can't see it, he is working. This is hope. ✳

CHAPTER 11

QUESTIONS AND EXCUSES

Giving Up, Giving In, or Giving Over

Confession and Repentance

IF YOU GREW up in church, you are probably familiar with these words, *confession* and *repentance*, and they probably feel *heavy*. The idea of confession and repentance gives new meaning to familiar misery, as the pair were often presented as a threat: confess and repent, or else. If you don't, something terrible is going to happen.

For me, confession became a list to capture on paper. I'd get out my journal and start to think of all the things that may have upset God. Maybe I said a bad word, had a bad thought, or lost my temper. I'd try to list everything I had done wrong, thinking God would dole out his grace, one sin at time.

Some of you grew up in traditions where you would go into a dark booth and tell someone you couldn't see everything you had done wrong that week. They absolve you, and then you go on your merry way. Or maybe you grew up in other traditions where you went down to the front of your church to pray with the pastor or to a youth camp where you burned a stick in the campfire to represent your bad decisions. With your confession, you were good to go until the following Sunday—or the following summer.

Our confessions are lists of what we have done, but the list often serves as a reminder of what we keep doing. We keep recalling the lie that we're not cut out to be any different, and that familiar refrain lurks in the back of our minds, underneath all the new resolve.

Guilt often drives our confession and repentance, and it begins to look a lot like karma.

You think you'll have to pay if you keep doing what you have been doing, so you promise to never, ever do it again. But when confession becomes a list, repentance becomes a promise. So let me ask you this: How has that worked out for you? How many times have you made that promise? How many times have you kept it?

Something New Is Something Now

The way of Jesus seems a little different. Instead of "repent or else," Jesus turns repentance into a response to good news, not the threat of bad news.

Repentance doesn't look like a promise not to do that again.

Repent means "to return" or "to change your mind," to literally change direction from the path you were going.

Repentance says, "I'm turning in a new direction, and I'm going to walk in the new way!"

(Ding, ding, ding! Did you catch that? This is what God has been doing *the whole time*.)

Often we get into patterns where we are stuck holding on to what we mistakenly believe are our core identities, either our glory days or our worst moments. This diminishes our vision, and it causes us to miss what's happening—the very thing we're actually invited to be a part of. To repent is to walk in a new way, to step into the life you've been invited to.

Confession means "to agree." Confession is not the task of making a list of the things to repent from, the things you've done wrong that you promise not to do again. And your agreement is not: "God, I agree these things are bad because they have caused a lot of trouble in my life." No, you confess so you can bring things into the light, so you may align your heart with God's heart, and seek what he desires for you. We aren't trying to earn God's forgiveness by the sincerity of our confession, but rather we receive what he has done because we trust what he has said. Rather than trying to

> TO REPENT IS TO WALK IN A NEW WAY, TO STEP INTO THE LIFE YOU'VE BEEN INVITED TO.

prove ourselves, we are bringing these things in the light so *we* can see. That's what confession is.

So, instead of a list and a promise, repentance is a return. Confession becomes the way we encounter the sustaining grace of our heavenly Father.

Jesus invites you to walk in his kingdom right now—today. He invites you to turn to something that has been made available to you, and your repentance points you in that direction—today.

Grace in this Moment

God's grace doesn't come to us one sin at a time, like coins in exchange for candy in a vending machine. It also doesn't work like a bank account, with savings and compounding interest, just waiting to be cashed in when we might need it. But grace does come in time.

Grace is both infinite and profoundly small. So small as only to be sufficient for this moment, like a breath. It can come to us in complete stillness, such that we don't even notice we're receiving it, and it is also available in the gulp of our desperate gasp, when we know it's the very thing that will save our lives.

I love to think about grace like this.

Consider this: you know you need to breathe. But you don't think about it, and you certainly don't obsess about it. When you went to bed last night and when you woke up, you were not gasping around hoping there would be air to breathe. It was available.

But if someone were to cover your nose and mouth so you cannot catch a breath, that someone might get punched in the face because you will fight to the death for breath.

God's grace, which defies the limits of time, comes *in* time.

Time carries this infinite, life-giving source.

Just breathe that in.

You've probably heard people say, "Time heals all wounds." We have heard it so often that now we nod our head and agree. When we are wounded, we nod our head and hope it's true, desperately so.

But remember, time doesn't heal. Time may provide enough space for amnesia to set in. The suggestion of time as a healer leaves us thinking you will get over something. That is foolish, and it actually undermines the promise of God. God's promise is redemption, and in redemption there is no need to get over or minimize or pretend. Instead of getting over the scars and trying to pretend they don't affect you, redemption brings the hard things into the story. Redemption makes them become useful for who we are to become.

Time doesn't heal. Grace heals. And time carries grace.

One of Jesus' closest disciples wrote a letter helping people process all that was happening around them. Peter wrote about how the mercy we find in Jesus awakens us to this available "living hope" (1 Pet. 1:3). In this letter he warns us to think carefully and to be aware of what is happening around us, to "set [our] hope on the grace to be brought to [us] when Jesus Christ is revealed" (1 Pet. 1:13).

Theologians call this future grace. John Piper summarizes this concept: "What I have in mind when I say 'future grace' is the grace we'll receive at the Second Coming and the grace that is arriving every moment as I move into the future."[6]

I love those words: *arriving every moment as I move into the future.* Just like breath. What an incredible picture. Grace is sufficient *for* the moment, *in* the moment.

The apostle Paul experienced this in the middle of a desperate struggle. Something bothered him so deeply, he desperately prayed for relief. He recalls begging God to take away this "thorn in [his] flesh" (2 Cor. 12:7). He describes it as something that troubles him, keeping him from something beautiful that lies ahead.

This is often what the sting of our past feels like. A thorn. Deeply imbedded. Painful. And everything we do is met with the sting of the pain, reminding us again and again of regret or shame or inadequacy, robbing us of hope. We beg for this to go away.

What we find is what Paul found. God doesn't just send answers to our requests. He sends something more powerful. God is working to redeem, which means he takes the things that are intended to hold us back and undermine us, and he uses them to create a beautiful future that is fueled by grace. He brings us grace in those most troubled moments where we are desperate to get out from where we are.

Just as Paul begged God to take away the thorn in the flesh, we beg God to take away the pain or the struggle we hold onto. Just like Paul, we pray, "God, if there is any way, take this away from me."

Paul didn't find relief; he found grace, and he wrote, "[His] grace is sufficient" (2 Cor. 12:9). Just enough. Precisely what was needed, as needed.

This requires us to trust. Deeply. We confront the uncertainty of the future by finding grace in the moment. This requires surrender.

A New Way to Surrender

Surrender is another one of those words that carries heavy baggage in the church. Surrender is like confession and repentance all rolled into one and then handled at youth camp or at the end of a church service. Surrender is our effort to stop doing things, and it is a reaction to the things we might regret. Surrender always feels like God taking away the things we think will be fun. It sounds like giving up.

In a way it is. But in another way, it isn't. (When I discovered this, I felt free. I want that for you.)

The verse that usually accompanies a sermon on surrender is found in Paul's letter to the Romans, the first verse in chapter 12.

> Therefore, I urge you, brothers and sisters, in view of God's mercy, to offer your bodies as a living sacrifice, holy and pleasing to God—this is your true and proper worship.
> (Rom. 12:1)

Holy. Acceptable. Oh boy, those are big words with high expectations.

For years this call to sacrifice bothered me. It made me afraid I was going to miss out on something. I felt like, if I gave myself to God, he would take away the one thing I enjoyed, the one thing I really wanted, the one thing I could control.

So I've got to offer my body as a sacrifice to God, and I've got to get myself right in order to do this. This is how we read, teach, and understand this verse all the time. We surrender to make ourselves holy, and we surrender to make ourselves acceptable.

We see those words "in view of God's mercy," and we think it's like a transaction. If he has done so much to make mercy available to me, then I should work my tail off to give up everything I can think of to pay for that mercy. But what if we thought about it differently? What if sacrifice is not about what I give up but rather what I'm willing to make available to God? Surrender isn't just what you give up; it is what you make available.

Remember what we learned about grace, that it comes to us like breath—in this moment, for this moment. Now consider the same provision of God's mercy: it is new every moment, in this moment, and is enough for this moment. To surrender is to make ourselves available to God's grace in this moment.

The conclusion of the past happens in the moment we meet grace for the next moment. This is where endurance becomes hope. We discover that we can endure because there will always and forever be enough grace for the moment we are in. Our hope sustains to the next moment, knowing grace will come like breath.

Have you ever had a moment when you knew God was with you? You sensed his presence; you believed so deeply. You felt free. His will and his way actually had authority in your life. It's a glorious moment, and you want to hold on to it forever.

Maybe it was sitting in a church service, walking on the beach, or perhaps reading this book. You took a breath and believed. You trusted and you actually felt hope. You sensed victory, and for a moment anxiety did not rule your thoughts. Depression gave way. All the things that drag you into the past patterns that leave you imprisoned and terri-fied of the future gave way to hope. That is because you were available to grace—God's amazing grace—in that moment.

Almost as soon as that happens though, you think, *Okay, I feel it now, but what about tomorrow? What about an hour from now?* And as you start worrying about the future, the floodgates open to those terrifying emotions, and soon you are drowning once again in all the things you hoped would be forever finished. This is the cycle that keeps so many people stuck and mired in fear.

Here's what I want you to know: in that moment when you felt God so near to you, you thought all your problems were solved. The truth is, the problems were not solved, but you were available for grace.

Instead of rushing out of that moment and worrying about the anxiety to come, and instead of being consumed with whether fear will rear its head again in the future, breathe in the grace of this moment. Fear will raise its head again. You will be tempted once again to do the thing you don't want to do. But sufficient grace will be available in the moments to come, precisely when you need it—in the moment, sufficient for the moment.

> SUFFICIENT GRACE WILL BE AVAILABLE IN THE MOMENTS TO COME, PRECISELY WHEN YOU NEED IT—IN THE MOMENT, SUFFICIENT FOR THE MOMENT.

To repent is to return. We return again and again until we remain returned. ✽

CHAPTER 12

LIVING REORDERED

Staying Faithful in the Process

Impatient with Process

A LOT OF us have a picture in our head that everything should be fine now. We receive Jesus, and we become new, and everything has changed. And then we feel puzzled when we still struggle with the things we used to struggle with.

We think of our lives as a fixer-upper show, like our spirituality is a transformation similar to the work of Chip and Joanna Gaines. We watch the fixer-upper process happen as the viewer, but the homeowners don't see the process. When the homeowners come back to see the transformation of their home, there's this grand unveiling. The curtain drops, and all is made new.

A lot of us think this is what happens with surrender and redemption, like it all happens in one giant moment of making new. Somehow you're supposed to just open your life, let the proverbial Chip and Joanna come in and work their magic, and—*voila!*—you're completely fixed. You let Jesus in, and he fixes everything immediately.

Let's consider what it looks like for transformation to really happen in your life. How do you actually become the person God has called you to be and created you to be? How do we navigate this reordering? I think this may be the toughest part. After all, we were all under one rule, and we're learning to live under a new rule—as those who are forgiven.

What does this look like?

When we don't change the way we think we should, or when it takes longer than we think it should, we just decide we are not cut out for this.

Let's take, for example, eleventh-grade algebra.

Eleventh-grade algebra is no joke. *Parenting* through eleventh-grade algebra might be even harder. No matter how good our day had been together, no matter how kind my tone toward my daughter, one question threatened to unravel even the best of days. I mean, it felt like a reasonable math-related question. But inevitably, every single time, one question would send everything off the rails: "Where is your scratch paper?"

You see, the night would usually go something like this. I'd go into her room to say good night, usually long after her bedtime, but I knew she was still awake. Because I'm a girl dad, I made a habit of closing out her day by telling her she's beautiful and that I love her. I'd walk into her room to find her working on her computer, plugging away on a homework assignment.

"Hey, kid, just wanted to say good night."

"Okay, Dad, just finishing up my algebra, and then I'm heading to bed."

(It still amazes me that you can do algebra on your computer.)

She would add, "Hey, Dad, just one quick question. Do you know how to do this problem?"

A daughter can never get too old for her dad to want to answer that question the right way. I was pretty good at algebra back in the day. And although I might be a little rusty, I'd feel up for the challenge.

I'd scoot up next to her and ask: "Where is your scratch paper?"

She would burst into tears. Immediately. Every time.

Listen, I never intended to exasperate my children. I've read Ephesians right along with you, and I know that's not what we're supposed to do. But I'm also pretty sure that "asking a reasonable question" does not qualify as "exasperation." I tried to be gentle and kind and understanding, but there are only so many ways you can ask about scratch paper. I mean, how can anyone do algebra without it?

I tried to explain that I needed to see her work. Then I tried to explain that I needed to see *my* work. She just looked at the screen, through tears, trying to determine what the right answer might be.

I was looking at the screen trying to determine the answer as well. But in order to determine the answer, I needed to find it. And in order to find it, I needed a piece of scratch paper.

Frustration. Tears. More frustration.

Then she would say, "I can't find the answer."

To which I would say, "Of course you can't, because you need a piece of scratch paper!"

The answer is not something you just find. A process is required.

Looking at our circumstances and hoping we'll *know* something we don't yet know is not an effective way to *understand* things we don't yet know. Learning is a process, and you need to show your work.

Otherwise, we stare off into the unknown, and we are easily paralyzed by what we don't know. It is easy to throw up our hands in frustration and declare, "I can't find the answer."

When we can't figure it out, we just decide we are not cut out for this.

Declarations of uncertainty paralyze us. They quickly become excuses for not moving ahead. Even worse, they actually become the reasons our past continues. As we overidentify, our struggle only grows.

When you try to do math but you can't, you end up saying, "I'm just not a math person." Granted, it isn't that big of a deal not to be a math person. But imagine when the struggle isn't about math but a question about your identity.

We tend to think the defining answer is to quit doing this or begin doing that, and we create a bulky list of promises in a stuttered series of starts and stops until we finally resolve, "Well, I guess this is just the way I am."

This way of thinking and attempting to grow needs to be concluded if we are to understand who we are: we are forgiven.

But we need to learn to live as those who are forgiven.

Living as Forgiven

Every once in a while, I like to eat out by myself. Not sure if you have ever done that, but I recommend it. When I was younger, I was terrified of this, mostly because of what other people in the restaurant might think. They could look at you and think to themselves, *Poor guy, no one would eat with him.* The idea of dining alone could bring back terrible memories of middle school when you couldn't find a single friend to eat with you. But now I can enjoy heading to a restaurant and requesting a table for one.

Here's what it looks like: you sit down and look over the menu. You take a deep breath and prepare to enjoy a meal all by yourself. (If you're an introvert, you're feeling really good about this mental picture right now.)

You place your order and receive the meal. When you're finished, your server approaches, and you know the drill—you're ready to pay the check.

But imagine this. What if she says, "Your meal has been taken care of."

You look around the restaurant, trying to figure out who did this. Is this a bad joke? Is somebody setting you up to get arrested? What's happening here?

As long as you remain there at the table, nothing has really changed. Nobody expects you to pay your bill while you're still sitting there. It's when you leave that they start to ask questions. You can sit there with the knowledge of your bill being paid, but the only way to experience the reality of this is for you to get up and walk out of the restaurant. To get up from your seat, walk past the other guests and servers, open the door, and wait for someone to tackle you for a "dine and dash." For a while, you keep one eye over your shoulder as you walk to your car, waiting for someone to catch up to you and tell you it was all a joke, all a mistake, all an error in your understanding. It's not until you get in your car and drive away that you begin to feel the freedom of your bill being paid.

That's the picture of what it looks like to live as one who is forgiven. Some of you are still sitting at the table, holding the knowledge in your head but afraid to leave the restaurant. You're wondering how this can be true, how it happened, and how it works, instead of learning how to walk in this freedom.

When we struggle, we get disappointed. We think we have to offer more to earn his favor and to experience life change. And so, we try to offer more of ourselves to beat the system. We don't learn how to actually live under the rule of his love, to live in forgiveness as one who has been forgiven, as one who owes God nothing but love and gratitude.

This is where rituals and reordering become necessary.

The Challenge of Reordering

I'm not a traditional guy, but there are a lot of things I've come to appreciate about the rituals of faith. As I learn more, rituals have become more important to me. Rituals can be as formal as Communion or baptism, or as casual as a cup of coffee or a walk by the ocean. A ritual is anything that causes us to take a step out of the pace of our lives and intentionally choose to remind ourselves of what is true, what matters, what means something to us. Rituals allow us to wage war against the tendency to return to the way things were.

Rituals remind us who we were made to be, and they remove the pressure from continually questioning who that is. They invite us to be present in this moment, and they allow us to experience the reordering of our lives.

The New Testament book of Hebrews addresses the tension of the old way and the new way:

> Day after day every priest stands and performs
> his religious duties; again and again he offers
> the same sacrifices, which can never take
> away sins. But when this priest had offered for
> all time one sacrifice for sins, he sat down at
> the right hand of God. (Heb. 10:11–12)

You may have read that verse before, and it may have felt like algebra to you. There's so much there that I don't want us to miss.

May I ask you a question? *Where's your scratch paper?*

There is a fundamental difference between the old way and the new way.

> In the old way, there were multiple priests.
> In the new way, there's a new priest: his
>   name is Jesus.

> In the old way, the priests brought multiple
>   sacrifices year after year.
> In the new way, Jesus made one sacrifice for
>   all sins, for all time.

> In the old way, the people met God halfway.
> In the new way, God came *all the way* to the
>   people.

In the old way, we met God in a temple.

In the new way, we *became* his temple.

The old way could never make us perfect.

The new way has made us perfect forever.

The old way was a transaction to please God.

The new way is an invitation to trust God.

When the priest finished his work of sacrifice, he would say, "It is finished."

When Jesus died on the cross, he said, "It is finished."

It is concluded.

That's a big deal. Don't miss it. It means you don't have to keep trying to offer something more to get him to do what he has already done. It means that you can get up, and you can walk in the freedom that your bill has been paid.

This calls for a new way of living, a reordering of our lives.

When we offer ourselves to God, it is not about our behavior being approved. It is about our entire life being made available. It's not an attempt to earn God's approval; it's a grateful response to his approval that Christ earned for us. This call to obedience isn't just a test to see if you measure up. It's an invitation to experience God and to become the people he has created us to be.

We don't get to experience this while we're still sitting in the chair at the restaurant, trying to wrap our minds around obedience and sacrifice. The understanding of who he is and who he has made us to be becomes real when we get up and walk in the freedom of that truth, that holiness we were created for.

Made Perfect, Being Made Holy

> For by one sacrifice he has made perfect forever those who are being made holy. (Heb. 10:14)

Let's consider those last words: "those who are being made holy." Don't read past that too quickly. You have probably heard it before, and I don't want the familiarity to cause the freedom of redemption to slip right past you. One sacrifice—Jesus on the cross—has *made you perfect forever.*

You have been made free.

You have been made whole.

You have been forgiven.

Your bill has been paid.

This is the ongoing nature of the transformation, the already and the not yet. The reason for rituals is reordering—getting us back into this rhythm of transformation and freedom. We are living in our holiness, and yet we are being made holy. It's now, and it's not yet.

I believe there is a moment when we receive what he has done for us—an actual moment when he has made us holy. We call it being born again, getting saved, confessing our sins, and accepting his sacrifice. And I believe this is also an ongoing process, something that happens over a lifetime. It's an ongoing, lifelong process of surrender, of becoming who we are created to be.

Those of us who have trusted him have been made perfect, and now we are *being* made holy. We are increasingly more and more holy as we submit to his way and authority in every area of our lives.

There are moments when we are open and available to God's leading. We trust so deeply. But there are also moments when the temptation to grab the reins and take control is overwhelming. We can all probably identify seasons where we were less faithful—or perhaps even faithless. This isn't about how well you behaved but about how much authority God held in your life, how much you were willing to trust him in the uncertainty of the new season. How much you would depend on the new mercies as you encounter new challenges in your life.

But it always comes back to drawing the same conclusion. When you most want to go back to the way things were, you have to say, "Right here, in this moment, God has authority. His will is being done here, now, in this moment, in my life."

Have you had a moment like that? Where you knew he was there, and you were forgiven, and it was all right? And what happened next? Probably you sinned a few minutes later. Or you messed up big time a few days later. Sometimes free people don't act like free people. Sometimes holy people don't act like holy people. Why didn't that moment last? Why couldn't we feel that forgiveness in the moments to come?

Because we only get sufficiency and sustaining grace in each moment, for that moment. The same grace that was available to you in the moment when you felt so confident? That grace is available in the moment to come.

Remember, grace is like breath. When you focus on your breath, you are focusing on this moment. Rituals do the same thing: they bring you into this moment.

How Rituals Work

A ritual can be anything that calls us out of the pace of our lives, to let God remind us who he is, what he's done, and what he has made available to us.

We don't just need to be reminded. We also need to experience it. This is where rituals matter. In rituals, we actually experience the reality that has been made available.

Let me explain. One of my rituals is a walk on the beach. I do this when I discover I'm striving too hard, when I need

God to calm me. Sometimes the pattern I need to break isn't bad or wrong, but I need to reorder how I'm processing things. I need to reorder my own life around dependence on him. Those familiar patterns I tend to lean on need a little disruption, especially when it is a particularly stressful season or I've got a lot on my mind.

The beach is one of my favorite places on the planet, and I don't take anything along to distract me. No phone, no pens, no journals. I do this to get alone with God because I need his peace. I don't need insight or direction, even though that is often the thing I feel like I need. I really just need the peace that comes with his presence. And so I walk. The actual process of my feet in the sand, of walking next to the water, is a ritual.

At first, I find myself wanting answers. I long for my journal or pen to write something down. But not having anything forces me not to concern myself with what I am demanding. This ritual is not for that. And after some time, I can feel myself begin to settle. I carve some time and make some space, not to prove to God I am serious about finding his presence and his peace but simply to reset and receive.

In this ritual I am actually experiencing something. My life is reordered in those moments.

And guess what happens: in those moments *I experience his peace.*

When we actually allow ourselves to experience the reality of God's sustaining grace, hope becomes real.

Rituals serve to reorder.

They serve as a tool to give us space to encounter God.

In that space he changes us. ✱

PART FOUR

HOPE FINDS ITS FOOTING

Redemption requires patience, which is exactly what hope looks like.

Conclusions allow us to live in the moment without being imprisoned by our past or paralyzed by the future.

CHAPTER 13

TAKE A BREATH

Experiencing Freedom from a Piled-Up Past

I HAVE A vivid memory of my childhood, and I remember the face and the name of my first girlfriend. I was in seventh grade, she was in eighth, and she was a cheerleader. I remember thinking she was way out of my league, and I clearly remember thinking I had no business liking her.

Let me tell you what it was like back in the day of dating before social media, just in case you're reading this and you weren't there. Back in the day, we couldn't stalk anyone online, and we had to do our own networking. We had to have our people talk to her people, to predict what would happen if we made a move.

I found out, through her people and mine, that if I said hi to her, she would say hi back. That's the first step, and once she says hi, you have clearance to move forward. In order to make the relationship "official," you have to ask her this question: "Will you go with me?" It's kind of a proposal. She'll say yes or no, or "I'll think about it."

("I'll think about it" means no.)

I asked the question, and she said yes, and suddenly we were in a relationship. And that's when the pressure was *on*.

Turns out, there were implications and expectations I was unaware of.

First, I had to walk her to her class. So I learned her schedule, I compared it to mine, I met her outside of her classroom, and I walked her to class. We'd get to her classroom, and I'd sprint back to the other side of the school, sweaty, but just in time not to get a tardy.

The next day I learned I was supposed to hold her hand. If I didn't hold her hand, I heard she would break up with me. I had never held a girl's hand before! I remember being unsure of where the fingers go. Do we interlock them? Is it palm to palm? What is the expectation? I knew I had to get it right.

Every day there was a new rule. Every day I wondered if I was doing enough. And on the sixth day, she broke up with me. Just like that.

She never talked to me again, and I had to live with the reality that she may have broken up with me because I didn't do enough of the right things. I didn't even know what I didn't know.

The continuing discovery of new rules and new expectations only added to the pressure. I was in a relationship that I didn't feel worthy to be in, and I was doing my best to perform to the level of expectation. Trying to be worthy of a relationship is exhausting.

This is how some of us live in our relationship with God. Chronically plagued by our sense of unworthiness and living out of our league, we try week after week, day after day, hoping we've done enough, hoping that our offering, our sacrifice, is acceptable. The cruelty of the brokenness in this world is that there is never enough. There is no such thing as enough. You'll always be hanging by a thread, wondering if this is the mistake that gets you rejected or abandoned.

Running from the Fat Man

When you drag your past along with you, it begins to pile up like snowpocalypse traffic on the highway (which in the south *literally* means simply the prediction of snow). Eventually one thing crashes into another, and it can feel impossible to navigate a way out. So we try to stay ahead of it all, to never let it catch up so it can't pile up. I think that's why a lot of people are as aggressive as they are: they've just been running forever.

I had a friend who stumbled onto a fitness plan. He was a self-described "big guy," and he lost more than a hundred pounds. He did it by running every single day. Like Forrest Gump, he just ran. He affectionately called his workout "Running from the Fat Man." That was his drive, the name for his motivation. He felt pressure to stay ahead of it all, and he kept running to stay ahead of "him." He ran hundreds of miles, but he felt like he could never stop.

There is increasing tension when we are running from the past and running into the future. The pace gets faster and faster, and our past continues to trail us if we don't draw it to conclusion. We end up trying to do things in an effort to live, but it ends up in some kind of grind.

We try to manage our fear of the future by controlling it. We try to obey our way into God's favor, hoping he will provide some relief from the paralyzing fear we have for the future. We tend to think that the more pleased God is with us, the better our lives will go. This is actually the prison of the past and the crushing pressure of the law.

When this is our thinking, we never get to enjoy the future because we can never find satisfaction in the present. Like my experience dating the cheerleader, the rules keep changing, and we're only ever chasing after a moving target, hoping we've done enough to merit God's favor.

That makes Leviticus important. (What? Back to that? I know. Stay with me.) Here's why.

The ancient culture had methods for appeasing their many gods. It's not that hard for us to imagine this in ancient culture. When one farmer needed rain, and then he saw his neighbor doing a dance, and the rain came the next day? Well, that's how a rain dance began.

What are other people doing to make the gods happy? What should I do, also?

Sometimes this got tragically dark and wicked. Some cultures even offered children, if that seemed to be what the gods wanted. They were forever offering something to make the gods happy again.

Sacrifice is an attempt to get what we want. The higher the stakes, the greater the sacrifice.

There are still places today where that happens. Times and customs have changed—thankfully—but this kind of god pleasing isn't crazy outside our realm of thinking.

We have all kinds of ways to try to manage or manipulate the future in our favor. If you're at somebody's house watching a football game, and you say something like, "Oh, this kicker's automatic," and then that kicker misses the field goal, I'll tell you what happens: the people won't invite you back. You're bad luck for that team. They're trying to appease the gods of football, and your presence is something they need to sacrifice.

We do this in lots of ways.

We have our list of things we should do—or not do. Most of us could write that list down right now, a list of actions that would make us holy and pleasing. But we need a different way to think about this.

Trying to Obey Our Way into the Future

When we read the Old Testament, the making of the Ten Commandments, we have this idea that Moses went up on the mountain and received the laws from God in one conversation. But it looks like there were probably six to eight exchanges between Moses and God, and they were designed to organize God's people to live faithfully within his covenant. They started with a top ten, and then immediately more laws were added until there were more than six hundred. If we look closely, it seems that the laws were created in response to what was happening in the community of God's people.

That's actually how a lot of laws and rules get made today; we have a new law because we found a loophole in an old law, and it turns out we need a new one. Rules are made in response to our ability to make loopholes in the laws that exist. At the core of it all, there are really only a few key laws, but more laws have to be added for clarity, to keep people from finding excuses to break the key ones. This is how rules change and evolve: people find a way around them.

Consider this one. A friend of mine has three teenage sons, and she had to implement a new rule: no pizza balling. I bet you didn't even know that was a thing, right?

Imagine what happens when you order pizza for three teenage boys: they are like vultures. There are fists, a lot of trash talk, and the pizza is a demolished mess.

Okay, new rule. You can only grab one slice of pizza at a time. A clear rule.

And they respond with the next question: When can we get our second?

Okay, new rule. You may not grab the second slice until the last bite of the first slice is in your mouth. Clear.

And they responded as teenage boys do: ball it up, shove the whole thing in their mouth, and grab the next piece.

Okay, new rule. No pizza balling.

That's how it happens. You have to keep making laws on top of laws in order keep up with the loopholes. I mean, pizza balling—who would have thought?

We not only create loopholes; we also create new laws in the way we treat one another and the things we are capable of doing to one another. Look at this list in Leviticus. Some of these are obvious and make perfect sense.

> Do not defraud or rob your neighbor. (Lev. 19:13)

> Do not hold back the wages of a hired worker overnight. (Lev. 19:13)

These are good. Don't take stuff that isn't yours. Do what you say you will do. I get it. I like this. But then there are laws like these:

> Do not curse the deaf. (Lev. 19:14)

> Do not . . . put a stumbling block in front of the blind. (Lev. 19:14)

What? What had to happen for these rules to become necessary? Who was yelling at the deaf and putting rocks in front of blind people?

Let's even look at the basics of the Big Ten. People look at the Ten Commandments as if they are the highest form of morality a human being can achieve. Think about this. If you have to come and tell people not to kill one another, something has seriously gone off the rails. A law that says don't kill—isn't this a basic rule for human beings? These are not high standards.

Most people have grown-up thinking that if you do good things then God will be good to you. Like a middle-school relationship, follow the rules and everything will go well. But if you break a rule, you'd better be ready to make it up or prepare yourself for a breakup.

And so we try to be good. And when we aren't as good as we think we ought to be, we promise to go to church or give some money or serve someone less fortunate. We profusely apologize, swear we will do better, and make some offer we think will make God happy.

This doesn't even begin to cover the inherent difficulty of determining whether you've kept just the first Ten Commandments. Now you can surely tell if you have killed someone or stolen something. But how do you know if you honored your parents—enough? Or worshipped God— enough? Is it safe enough to say "gosh darn" as a substitute for taking his name in vain, or is that another loophole?

Continuing a system of laws—and loopholes to laws—
will never be enough to experience the life God has for us.
This system could never fully free your heart to trust because
there is a haunting feeling that you haven't done enough.

The book of Hebrews lays this out, explaining that the
new way is not a continuation of the old way, nor is it a com-
bination of the new and the old. It is something entirely different. The old is "set aside," "weak," and "obsolete" (Heb.
7:18; 8:13). The language used in the Bible to describe this
distinction is jarring.

Here are a couple of places where we see this contrast.
Let's read it together:

> The former regulation is set aside because
> it was weak and useless (for the law made
> nothing perfect), and a better hope is intro-
> duced, by which we draw near to God. (Heb.
> 7:18–19)

> For if there had been nothing wrong with
> that first covenant, no place would have
> been sought for another. (Heb. 8:7)

> By calling this covenant "new," he has made
> the first one obsolete. (Heb. 8:13)

The old way leaves us longing, but God has introduced
to us a better hope in which we trust him enough to come to
him. The new covenant was necessary precisely because the

old one did not work. It could never make us right and never set us free. We were never designed to follow rules but rather to experience the fullness of his love and life as we live in a relationship with him, receiving his grace and trusting his love. Our obedience is not a way to earn God's favor, but we offer our lives as an expression of it.

By calling it "obsolete," the author of Hebrews makes clear that the old way no longer has authority over us. The new covenant was established by the once and for all sacrifice of Jesus. We have been transferred into his kingdom, and we live under his loving rule. This way of life doesn't just require our compliance to the law but the allegiance of our hearts.

Our tendency to return to the old way of thinking is so instinctive and natural to us. The new way of life under the new covenant requires incredible attention and moment by moment dependence until we learn to receive his grace with the same way we receive our breath.

Take a Breath

I am a certified scuba diver. Now that doesn't mean much because I don't actually dive. But I took the course and went through the training, and it is one of the coolest things ever. Life underwater is incredible. The peace and serenity. The beauty, as you linger weightless in another world. All this is available . . . if you can get past the tendency to panic.

Our training began in a classroom, learning about the equipment and the rules and dangers and the incredible experience that awaited us. Then we moved into the pool. And this is where I had to learn to breathe . . . and to trust.

You get your gear on—a mask to cover your eyes and nose, a tank of oxygen on your back, and the regulator in your mouth to deliver that oxygen so you can breathe. And then into the water you go, all the way to the bottom of the pool. You concentrate on breathing. In and out. Each breath you take, your regulator regulates the air you are breathing in, and then bubbles go everywhere as you exhale. The feeling is surreal. You are breathing underwater.

Once you are comfortable breathing underwater, the instructor introduces challenges and obstacles that might occur while diving and instructions on how to respond to them. One of the exercises we had to practice was taking the mask off your face and putting it back on, all while underwater. This is important because if your mask gets knocked off, you'll instinctively spring to the surface, and the immediate shift in air pressure could kill you.

So when it was my time, I sat on the bottom of the pool, ten feet under the water. I was relaxed and breathing just fine, finally comfortable breathing underwater. Then the instructor swam in front of me, and he gave me the signal: he put his hands on my shoulders. (This felt a little dramatic, but it proved important).

It was time to take off my mask.

I removed my mask, the water rushed in around me, and I suddenly knew why his hands were on my shoulders: he was teaching me to fight my instincts. I tried to jump off the bottom. The sensation of the water sent a wave of panic, and everything in me said, *Get to the surface now.*

But I'd forgotten one thing . . . one very important thing. I *could* breathe. I had taken off my face mask, but I was still wearing my oxygen. I had a source of air that I could trust, but I had to find my bearing and choose to trust it.

I managed to push through those moments of panic and remind myself to breathe through my mouth. And as soon as I did, I inhaled and then exhaled. I could breathe. Once I settled down, I could put my mask back on.

When the panic of the future seems overwhelming, we long to return to what we know—to shoot up to the surface. We have to remember we have a source of hope that can be trusted. We just have to stop and choose to trust it.

Maybe you need a friend to hold your shoulders to keep you from surfacing.

We need this space to remind ourselves that the old way has given way to something new. The source of this new way of life is found as we rest in the reality that a new way has been made. And that reality is found in a moment.

Like the air from the tank on my back, grace comes like breath. But with the unfamiliar rushing in around us, our tendency is to get back to what we've known. Instead, we hold still and remember we have a source we can trust. And we take a breath.

Taking a breath is finding a moment. Instead of doing more or offering more to be seen as holy and pleasing, we stop, we breathe, and we trust that what Jesus has done is enough. It is finished.

The old has gone. The new has come. And here is where hope and fear all meet in a moment. This is why surrender isn't just a promise. It is an end. We find the reality of freedom in a moment, where surrender is breath. ✳

Chapter 14

THE ULTIMATE CONCLUSION

The Freedom of Finally Finishing

Avoiding the Ending Concludes the Wrong Thing

MY OWN JOURNEY of faith has been marked by doubt. You might find that a little odd coming from a pastor because we are supposed to have it all figured out, and our answers must be sure.

Or perhaps you find it to be comforting.

I grew up with the assumption that doubt is bad. Doubt was a symptom of bad faith. Far too many people have lived under this idea, and their growing doubt became the end of their faith. An entire generation of people have walked away from their faith because of a college professor who dismantled the Bible in a way they couldn't reconcile. Faith seems to shrink as doubt grows.

Or perhaps your own questions ended your faith. Questions about violence, injustice, suffering, or your own personal struggle. Questions you didn't even feel comfortable enough to ask, let alone find an answer to.

And then there is a tendency to grab sure-fire answers to every question you might have. This ends up making matters worse because quick answers short-circuit the process required. What makes sense in your head doesn't take root in your heart.

And so you came to a conclusion.

And so did your faith.

Perhaps this is an opportunity for you to consider something different. Perhaps doubt isn't a bad thing. In fact, faith actually requires it. Perhaps your doubt could become the seedbed for curiosity and allow you to see something you could not imagine before.

My own journey of doubt becoming curiosity has given me greater hope than I imagined. The gospel of my childhood—with all of the good things and the bad things—has blossomed into a compelling promise worthy of my life.

So maybe you've concluded the wrong things, and it's time to bring that to an end.

What God Finished

So much of my understanding of the gospel shifted when I began to pay attention to what Jesus actually said—his actual message. When I read the New Testament through the lens of what Jesus *actually* said and did, things began to take a different shape.

Jesus talked about a kingdom—a rule. The kingdom is at hand, and we are invited to repent, to reconsider, to rethink, and to reorient our way into his. The more I began to understand that sin is far more about authority and allegiance than behavior, the more I began to realize what the gospel was about.

Far more than just a choice between heaven and hell, the message of Jesus was about life and death.

Jesus's message is an invitation to life with God, to live in the way we were created to live. We simply are not designed to find life apart from him. But this is precisely the sinful condition. We are separated from God. The Bible calls that death.

So the gospel—the good news of the birth, the life, the death, and the resurrection of Jesus Christ—does something. What does it do? Most of us have grown up thinking that gospel gets us to heaven. And that's pretty much all we know.

Too much happens along the way for this view of the gospel to sustain us and for us to experience and learn to live in his promised new mercies.

We need to finish one story in order to understand how it brings us the beginning of the

> JESUS'S MESSAGE IS AN INVITATION TO LIFE WITH GOD.

new one. This is exactly what Jesus said in his last moments before His own death.

It is finished.

These are the words Jesus proclaimed on the cross as he gave his life as the once and for all sacrifice for sin. This includes your sin and mine.

My own unraveling of the gospel has led me to see things I had never considered before. This is one of the great things you experience when you aren't trying to repeat what you learned long ago but instead continue to walk in the unfolding of God's mercy. You continue to learn and grow and become. It is frightening for sure but oh so freeing.

Coronation

Now I am not sure if you are up to speed on coronations, but I am. After all, I've watched *The Crown*. If you haven't seen this series, you should dive in as soon as you finish this book. You too can become a self-proclaimed coronation expert.

The Crown is the super popular binge-worthy show based on the British monarchy. It takes you back to the abdication of the throne that led to King George and then Queen Elizabeth. My wife and I loved it so much that we spoke to each other in British accents. I began referring to her as Her Majesty as I brought her coffee each morning.

There is one episode dealing with the coronation of King George (Elizabeth's father). It is spectacular, with all the pomp and circumstance you can imagine. There is a moving scene in which he is talking to his daughter, the future Queen Elizabeth, about the importance of the coronation.

The coronation is the moment when the sovereign assumes her rightful place. There is a royal entrance, a crown, and a throne. There is the ascension to the throne, where she will be hailed as sovereign.

If you haven't seen *The Crown*, perhaps you've seen *Frozen*. The coronation is the day Elsa is crowned, and this celebration is marked by "the first time in forever" that they have opened the gates. (Now this song is probably stuck in your head. You're welcome.) The people of Arendelle create a festival of pomp and circumstance as Elsa takes her rightful place.

When I went back and read the story of the crucifixion again, I began to realize that this story of death and resurrection is the story of the coronation of a King.

Consider this: When did Jesus take his rightful place? When did Jesus become King? Not sure I'd really thought about it before. I realized that I had some assumptions that had never been challenged because I had come to believe that kings don't lose; they win. So Jesus' reign began when he *rose*. Makes perfect sense.

My research led me down a fascinating rabbit trail and painted a beautiful picture of the gospel. The crucifixion was the ultimate conclusion.

Then I reread the account of Jesus' crucifixion recorded in all four Gospels. The story was the same as it always was, but I had to consider some details I'd never paid attention to. (My one word is *detail*, remember!)

The details leading to the crucifixion consist of the mockery of Jesus. You might be familiar with the crown of thorns, the reed, and the purple robe—all given to Jesus intended to make a mockery of this would-be, wanna-be king of the Jews. But just like God, he took what was intended to harm and belittle and undermine, and he brought it under the power of his promise of redemption. Their mockery becomes his coronation.

There was a procession, but instead of a mighty steed surrounded by soldiers, weapons, and the show of might, this King rode in on a donkey. That procession began a coronation no one would expect.

The Scriptures describe this upside-down way by saying God chose the foolish things and the weak things to undermine our hope in our own wisdom and strength and perspective (1 Cor. 1:27–29). Jesus' humble entrance on a mule begins the upside-down procession. His rod is a reed that he is beaten with, and his crown, made of thorns, is not designed to honor him but to hurt and belittle and torture. Everything was designed to humiliate and to punish. This sham of a scene became the coronation of the King. God chose the foolish things to reveal the kingdom things.

Just as Queen Elizabeth ascended the steps to take her throne, so did King Jesus. Up the hill, with his cross. He was nailed in place. The coronation of the King of kings.

His inaugural address is seven statements, and I want us to focus on three words:

It. Is. Finished.

Jesus brought the rule of oppression to a conclusion. It wasn't the oppressive rule everyone assumed. The death of this King served as the full and final sacrifice for sin. His sacrifice makes forgiveness available to everyone who would receive it, who would receive him.

As those who are forgiven, we live in the freedom of God's available kingdom. On the cross, God was reconciling the world to himself. His sacrifice is our forgiveness. Forgiveness is the way we are reconciled into the kingdom.

His death brought the oppressive rule of sin to a conclusion. And he took that rule to the grave.

His death sealed its fate. That's what death does.

Death Always Precedes Resurrection

Death is one of the great mysteries of life. There are peaceful transitions and tragic ends. Either way, there is a grief with death because it is the end of something and the beginning of a separation.

My son-in-law loves *The West Wing*. Hands down, his favorite president is Jed Bartlett. His passion for all things *West Wing* has eventually lured me into a weekend binge of Sam, Josh, CJ, and the crew. Somehow, when I can go to bed thinking that our country is in the hands of Jedidiah Bartlett, I can sleep at night.

The West Wing ran for seven seasons on network television in the early 2000s, and then the series was featured on Netflix for the next few years. It was recently been removed from Netflix, so you have to buy the DVDs in order to binge-watch now, which Carson has done. Nothing will stop him from time with the Bartletts. He has watched every season probably a dozen times, and he can identify almost any episode. He's only twenty-four-years-old as I write this, so if you count the episodes and do the math, he has spent a great deal of his young life in *The West Wing*.

But there is one thing about *The West Wing* that Carson avoids: he's never seen the final episode. He has never watched the grand finale, the conclusion of *The West Wing*. He refuses to watch the last episode because he doesn't want it to be over.

Have you ever felt like that about anything? Somehow we think if we avoid the end, we can keep the thing alive. The problem is, this just keeps us repeating the same episodes over and over. As soon as something looks like it may end, we circle back and restart the cycle. No big deal if this is *The West Wing*. But when it's your life that gets stuck, the reruns get old, and the future gets forsaken.

The hard thing about resurrection, though, is that it requires death.

The reality of our shameful past is that it needs to die. Its fate needs to be sealed. Otherwise, it continues its operative rule over our lives, paralyzing us in the moment, preventing us from receiving grace and experiencing its sufficiency.

The rule of sin has been defeated and our tendencies need to die.

But our tendencies are familiar.

For some, your past is the excuse to not trust anyone. It keeps you cynical and guarded. For others, your past keeps you motivated. You are outrunning the ghost—trying so hard not to be what you were, thinking if you can just get enough distance from it, everything will be fine.

Jesus makes an interesting observation, recorded in John 12:

> Truly, truly, I say to you, unless a grain of
> wheat falls into the earth and dies, it remains
> alone; but if it dies, it bears much fruit.
> (v. 24 ESV)

He is, of course, talking about his own sacrifice but also his death more generally. The seed cannot produce fruit, he says, unless it finds its finish, meets its conclusion. We can get this metaphor, even if we aren't farmers.

Seeds have to be planted. They get buried. And when they do, something new emerges. A tiny little seed produces hundreds of apples.

This is the way of sacrifice.

We offer ourselves. But there are patterns and habits we know need to end. We resolve to stop or quit, but that is not enough. They fall to the ground, but they don't die. But notice what Jesus says happens: if it doesn't die, it remains alone.

Alone. Disconnected. Separated.

What got finished on the cross was life apart from God. We no longer have to live promising to do better or obey more. You aren't doomed to what you've always done. Death is separation. The good news of the gospel is the end of death. No more separation from life.

The way of life isn't about your intentions or how guilty you feel about what you've done. The way of life is about the present, about you being present and available for what has been made available to you: his presence. He is the way, the truth, and the life, and because you cannot be separated from him, death has no sting and holds no power. The reign of sin and death met its

THE BEAUTIFUL THING ABOUT DEATH IS THE PROMISE OF THE RESURRECTION.

final conclusion on the cross. The crucifixion is the ultimate conclusion.

The beautiful thing about death is the promise of the resurrection. The things you allow to die give way to an unshakable hope of resurrection that rests on God's unshakable promise of redemption. ✳

CHAPTER 15

CAPTIVE PATTERNS

Creating Rhythms of Surrender

EAT. SURF. SLEEP. Repeat.

Lots of guys in my town wear shirts like this, and it's a slogan for the pattern of a perfect lifestyle. I have to agree, yes, I'd enjoy that life, too.

But none of us actually get to live in a pattern like that. Obviously. We get stuck in other patterns.

Even as I sit here on my back porch, feeling the pressure to bring this book to a conclusion, I am running through all sorts of thought patterns and drawing conclusions from them.

> *I am so excited about writing.*
>
> *I am so excited about this book.*
>
> *This book is no good.*
>
> *I am not a writer.*
>
> *Repeat.*

It is amazing the conclusions we draw when we're stuck in patterns. (I have concluded in this process that I'm much better at putting off writing than I am at writing.)

We get stuck in all kinds of patterns.

> *I'm a good parent. I'm a bad parent. Repeat.*
>
> *I'm a good spouse. I'm a bad spouse. Repeat.*
>
> *I feel hopeful. I feel hopeless. Repeat.*
>
> *This year will be different. This year is like last year. Repeat.*
>
> *Try harder. Try harder. Fail. Repeat.*

Old familiar patterns are concluded not by stopping them but by creating new patterns. It's hard for our brains, and it's hard for our hearts to consciously develop new patterns. But we must. The growth matters.

The good news is this: God is not glorified in your strength. He is glorified in his. The patterns that drive us are often ways in which we continue to try harder and make more fervent promises. This is the culmination of the continuation that needs to be concluded.

If we depend on our own strength, our own will power, to get our own way, we are likely to repeat the futile patterns that have long left us frustrated and chasing. But if our source is God's grace, we find there is sufficient power and strength. We can remain hopeful, and in that hope we can remain faithful. The beauty is that God's grace is found in his presence.

His Presence

When Jesus gives the promise of his comfort and the promise of his peace, it has nothing to do with some utopian view of our world or our perfectly controlled and comfortable circumstances. In fact, it is the opposite. He actually promises that in this world we will experience trouble (John 16:33). Our world is groaning, remember.

But he tells us to take heart because he has overcome this troublesome world. What a beautiful invitation. To take heart is the opposite of losing heart, to pull in the opposite direction of giving up or giving in. To take heart is to trust and believe and hold on at the precise moment you want to abandon your belief.

Jesus invites us right in the middle of the trouble and the hardship, right in the moment to take heart, to refuse to give in and instead to encounter Him.

Our resolve and commitment to continue gives way to rest and trust in the moment. His comfort and his peace are his presence. Nothing more. Nothing less.

"Take heart!" Jesus beckons, "for I have overcome the world."

Now, before you get a picture of Jesus coming off the third ring rope dropping an atomic elbow on anything and everything that stands between you and your comfort, we might need to consider that he ushers in a new way. Something more is available.

Jesus has overcome the world. That is what he said. But perhaps not in the way we think.

My first thought is a violent overthrow of everything that stands in my way. "He's overcome. That means nothing can touch me." Except it does. The trouble of the world not only touches me, but sometimes it feels like it crushes me.

Here is where our old thinking needs to find its conclusion.

When I think of the word *overcome*, it doesn't just mean "to conquer." We can also use it to talk about being overcome by emotion, which means that the emotion we feel touches and affects everything about us.

I wonder if we could say the same for Jesus. He touches and affects everything. There is nothing in my life that isn't affected by his touch, his presence.

In fact, there is nothing in this world that isn't affected by his touch, his presence.

He has conquered the way of life under which cycles of shame and fear and effort have been concluded. He has inaugurated a new way. He has overcome the world and has invited us to live in his available kingdom.

The process of feeling pressure to promise more, earn more—that has come to an end. Jesus has overcome. He affects everything. You have a new way, and it's for God's glory.

Grace and Presence: The Conclusion

We are created in the image of God—*imago Dei*. We have been transformed to the image in which we have been created by the sacrifice of Jesus Christ. The redemption story is the restoration of everything returned to reflect the glory of God.

This is the appointed conclusion.

This is a nice thought. My life for God's glory. I've said it, I've given messages on it, I believe it. But what are we talking about?

A lot of people live with the sense that they don't bring glory to God because they fear they don't do enough big things for God.

"It's not how it should be."

"How should it be?"

We don't know. We just assume that we're never doing enough.

Our hypercritical, calculating selves obsess over how the pieces of our lives are going to fit together into the puzzle we think fulfills his purposes and reflects his glory.

God's glory seems lofty . . . too lofty.

We see this sentiment throughout the Scriptures, that God's thoughts are higher than ours, his ways far above, and his plans loftier than we can imagine. He created an epic beginning, and he had an epic conclusion in mind.

This is the epic ending of all things. When we see Jesus face-to-face, all of these things are fully known.

There's a well-known story about Johann Sebastian Bach,[7] the world-famous composer.

I try to imagine the story going like this.

He's reading over every note. Fine-tuning the melody, each rest and fermata, carefully placed. I imagine many drafts and redrafts as he hums and thinks, listening to see if this feels right. I imagine the process being painstakingly tedious, the complexity of the composition and trying to get each part to fit into the whole.

Finally, it is finished.

And he signs off with three letters: S.D.G.

Soli Deo Gloria.

Glory to God alone.

You may have heard that before, but do you know what he often wrote at the beginning? Again, I try to imagine. Looking at the blank page. So much inside, so many questions and perhaps self-doubt and fear. Perhaps having finished his *Brandenburg Concerto No. 3*, he's moving onto the next project, getting ready to begin again.

It would be so easy to try to recreate what he already knows to be beautiful and enjoyable. And the pull to that familiar refrain draws hard. But something about what is to come draws him ahead. Unable to know how the future would unfold, the moment is pointed—the tension between the beauty of what is already behind him and the struggle to find what lies ahead. And in that moment, on the top of the blank page, he scribbles the Latin phrase, "*Jesu Juva,*" which translates, "Jesus, help!"

In that moment, he finds the grace to begin. And that grace is in the Presence of Jesus.

When we call out, "*Jesu juva,*" we cry out, "Jesus, help!" This is our surrender, and it happens in this moment. It doesn't need to wait until Sunday, or until next summer's trip to camp, or even until tomorrow's early morning devotional.

I don't see this as a last-ditch thrown-up prayer but rather an acute awareness that in this moment, in the face of the uncertainty of a blank page, there is a dependence on grace. Jesus, *help.*

Jesus, meet me here in this place. Meet me here with your sufficient grace.

Jesus, help, isn't like "Get me out of here," but rather *Jesus, come and be with me in here.*

A New Way to Surrender

I want us to consider a new way to surrender. I learned this from my years in student ministry working with high school and middle schoolers, and this has been confirmed in my years working with adults. Instead of measuring our surrender by commitment, intention, sincerity, or effort, I want us to consider the role of time in the way we surrender.

This is where I discovered the surrender interval. A surrender interval is the amount of time between points of surrender. Here is how it works.

Summer camps are a staple in student ministry, super fun and super effective. I know this firsthand, and I believe it is a critical part of helping students connect with God. Often the summer camp experience is described as a defining moment, the place or time where faith becomes real.

Summer camp is a moment of surrender. It is real. It is deep. But what happens? We come back from the mountaintop experiences, and the real world catches up. The old system that the rest of the world lives in takes hold, and before we know it, we end up back in the same patterns we'd tried to escape.

We tend to think our faith just didn't take. And then summer comes around again. Kids sign up, they go to camp, they encounter God, and this becomes a point of surrender. Again.

A whole year between summer camps.

It is real, again. It is deep, again. And this time we mean it, again.

That is a surrender interval of one year.

Too long, right? Of course.

So as a youth pastor, I planned retreats every three months. To reorder a student for a weekend or a week every three months created space for these defining moments. A point of surrender four times per year.

Genius, I thought. *Shorten that surrender interval.*

That makes a surrender interval of three months.

(I assume you see how this is working.)

Most of us try to create a habit of going to church every week. And each Sunday we show up with an entire week's worth of stuff, the continuing pileup of our past. Perhaps your experience is like mine. Every week you are mustering more sincerity, more intention, and more fervor. And so every week becomes a point of surrender.

This is a surrender interval of seven days.

And soon you learn that seven days is too long. So you commit to a daily devotion, reading your Bible every morning. For some, this becomes yet another streak to tend to or keep up with, right? But nevertheless, you find this to be a worthy discipline. And effective. And so every day, day after day, the morning becomes a point of surrender.

And your surrender interval is even shorter: twenty-four hours.

This is like the pinnacle of spiritual discipline. Reading your Bible and praying every single day. A point of surrender every single day.

Do you know what I have learned? Twenty-four hours is *way* too long!

You can open your eyes in the morning and breathe a prayer. "Lord, I surrender this day to you and for your purposes."

You are sincere. You mean it.

And then your kids get up, and the wheels come off your good intentions.

Or you get an email that makes you angry. Or you look at Facebook, and you're drawn into an argument. Or one thing out of a hundred pull you back into the old, familiar patterns.

We can't wait seven days to surrender again. We can't wait seven minutes. This is the miracle of his presence and potential of the moment. Surrender is available right here.

Surrender isn't a promise to change. It isn't mustering up willpower to do better.

Surrender is to rest in the reality of his presence and experience the reality of his promise in the moment. Our souls are filled with his grace the same way our lungs drink in life-sustaining oxygen—one breath at a time.

> Take a breath.
>
> Receive this gentle reminder to breathe.
>
> This reminder to breathe is an invitation to
>   surrender.
>
> Rise to receive.

We surrender to his grace in the moment as we breathe: *Jesu juva.* Jesus, help. ✳

MR. AUSTIN

MR. AUSTIN WAS the quintessential old man. Picture the toy doctor of *Toy Story* fame. Mr. Austin was always cast as the old man for any of our videos at Port City, so classic he was in every way. He had wrinkles that told endless stories and eyes that told you he cared deeply. His smile was wry, a grin that seemed to say, *There is more to come.*

When you put together the wrinkles, the eyes, and that smile, you get hope. Mr. Austin was hope.

He was perhaps the most giving man I've met. Generous with anything he had, but mostly he was generous with his presence. He was humble and gentle and unassuming.

Mr. Austin was my father-in-law.

His name is Owings F. Austin. He was named after the doctor who delivered him, Dr. Owings. I believe Francis was his first name, but he didn't like it that way so he changed it. I have known him since I was in the second grade, and I have always called him Mr. Austin.

After he and his wife were in a serious car accident, they moved in with us. Brenda recovered in the front living room, and Mr. Austin was set up with a recliner and a TV in the sunroom, which was really a hallway with windows. We eventually finished out our garage as a mother-in-law suite with a small living area, bathroom, and bedroom. We shared a kitchen, which is an important detail in this story.

Always unassuming, Mr. Austin never wanted to be in the way. He always wanted to earn his keep, to make sure he contributed, to be confident he had done his share. This is how he'd been raised. Even as he lived with our family, he was most comfortable with an assignment, so his job became the hardwood floors. Every day, usually around 5:45 in the morning, he'd get out the broom and dustpan to complete his duties. And—this is the best part—after sweeping, he'd mop with the Swiffer, like baby wipes for the floor. Boy, I'll tell you, he'd get going. He would be slumped over just so, to get the right amount of pressure to get the floors shiny. Mr. Austin never left a job half finished.

One December morning, he was "swiffering" the kitchen floor as I came in to get my coffee. I had poured two cups, doctored them perfectly, and I was just about to return to have coffee with my wife when Mr. Austin said, "Hey, Mike, you got a minute? I wanna tell you my word. I finally picked it."

Of course I did. His gentle invitation was a call to pay attention.

He hunched over the Swiffer handle and began to speak. His discourse would always begin the same way, with a story. This particular morning, I was going to hear about the last word he would choose.

You see, every December, Mr. Austin would pick a word for the following January and into the new year. (Let me say, it is humbling to have your father-in-law say your book changed his life—at sixty-eight years old![8] But he made sure I knew.) Each year he couldn't wait to tell me his new word, but he never wanted to tell me *just* the new word. He would always start at the beginning of his vast collection, recalling how he had chosen each word, and then he would conclude with the latest selection.

I set the cups down and settled in, and though the coffee cooled while I listened, I'll never forget that morning with him. He told me once again the entire journey through his eleven words, and it was a beautiful thing, even at six in the morning.

He walked me through *pride, grace, humility, gratitude, vision, discipline, finish, express, love, message, fullness*—each word a season, each season began as each season ended.

He carefully talked about each season, what he'd learned, what he sensed God was doing, and how he'd experienced God's faithfulness and learned to be faithful.

And then he said, "I picked my word for this year, Mike. My word is . . . hold on."

He set down the Swiffer and rushed to his room to get his Bible, thick and tattered, the cover torn off, but with writing on every page. He came back to the kitchen with his Bible open to the book of Psalms. He said, "Are you ready for this?"

Then he pointed, and he read to me Psalm 92:14. "They will still bear fruit in their old age."

His eyes lit up. He said, "My word is *fruitful*!"

Mr. Austin was eighty-one years old, and he still over-flowed with contagious excitement for the life he was given. With eight decades behind him, he still saw all the potential for new things to be born in his life and through his life. He still lived in the moment, expecting and anticipating God's faithfulness.

The thing is, Mr. Austin's life had not been easy.

He grew up through the Depression, with no real understanding of just how poor his family was. His father died before he was three years old. He later realized the unbelievable strength and unshakable faith of his mother as she worked hard to provide for her twin boys, Owings and Oliver.

His mom watched over them, working to provide and to protect them. Mr. Austin got his work ethic and his resiliency from her. At the age of fifteen, he had to endure the death of his twin brother, who drowned in a river they had been forbidden to swim in.

The death of his brother plunged him into a decade he called "the lost years," when he lost his ambition, goals, and hope. These years nearly brought the faith he'd been raised in to a conclusion.

His young wife (my mother-in-law) brought him back to the church, and he attended only to please her. But God can work with broken hearts, and he worked in Mr. Austin's. The Holy Spirit drew him near once again, and Mr. Austin's faith was fortified with the refined strength of something broken and made whole.

He could have fallen into a pattern of cynicism, shame, and disappointment. Instead, he resolved to find faith in the moment, and drew a conclusion to his fear.

After years of active duty in the army and a long career working for a large financial company, Mr. Austin discovered there were no small finance companies in his part of town, and he knew many people who needed small loans in order to survive. He retired from the large company, and he used his retirement benefits to start a business of his own—at age fifty-one.

GOD CAN WORK WITH BROKEN HEART.

This was a giant risk, later in life, especially for someone who had never been an entrepreneur. He started a finance company specializing in small loans. The mission of his little company was to be the working person's friend. So fitting for Mr. Austin. And that is exactly what he did.

Rather than aggressively lending and collecting to earn high interest and make money, he was a friend, working with each client to help them with whatever financial problem they faced, and helping people rebuild their credit. In an industry that is measured by the bottom line, Mr. Austin measured his success by the relationships he enjoyed. And he was successful. As he walked the streets of the city square, he was constantly greeted by many of the locals he'd helped.

He invested a lot of years in his community, lending money but mostly helping people. I am sure people thought of him far more as someone who would help than someone who loaned money.

He became a pillar in the community, keeping families and finances afloat. In the end, however, his business partner and stockholders sold the company out from under him, and Mr. Austin lost everything he had. This was a devastating blow to him and his family. After nearly fifteen years, his dream shattered, as he was undermined and betrayed.

Imagine being sixty-five and having everything you've worked for ripped out from underneath you.

This was a tough season, but he'd seen tough before. Instead of retreating into the coulda, woulda, shoulda's, Mr. Austin turned his attention, not to the past but also not to the future.

Instead, Mr. Austin learned the power of the moment and the grace available there. This grace had sustained him before, and he trusted it would sustain him now. His faith, his resolve to be faithful in the moment, brought him through.

Those circumstances would have been enough for some people to call it finished, but Mr. Austin wasn't done living— no way. He told me he couldn't stop thinking, *How can I give back? God has been so good to us.*

In essence, he started over at the age of sixty-five, and he enjoyed some of his most effective ministry. When most people begin to slow down, it seemed as though he was just getting started.

You can't find this if you spend your time trying to run from your past. You have to tie a bow on it. Each season needs a conclusion, for when it finds its finish, your past finds its use in God's promise of redemption.

He mentored so many young adults through addiction and into their marriages, businesses, and families. In fact, at the age of seventy, he was the best man in a wedding. The groom was in his twenties, and Mr. Austin stood next to him as his best man.

On his eightieth birthday, I read a card from two elementary schoolkids who wrote, "Thank you for teaching my daddy about the cross." People have dressed up as him for Halloween, and one of his young friends even named their son after him. He was legendary.

Each chapter of his life came to a conclusion, and each one became a foundation for the chapter to come. This required his past to be concluded. He did this by staying faithful in the moment, not ashamed of his past and never too afraid of his future.

He never stopped being faithful, and he never stopped trusting that God would be faithful to complete what he'd begun. Each of his chapters became even more powerful than the one before. The reason there was fruitfulness in his last chapter was because there was not futility in the earlier ones.

You see, the worst part of a dragging past is that it fuels futility. As time presses on, we begin to believe that the seasons to come have no point. No appointed purpose because it has not been assigned an appointed season. Mr. Austin refused to let the past drag him down, and he refused to let one single year—*or even one single day*—be rendered meaningless.

Mr. Austin suffered a stroke on August 23, 2019. He never regained consciousness, and he passed away eight days later. Over those eight days, countless people called and came by to see him, each one with a story to tell about how Mr. Austin had influenced their lives, how his fruitfulness benefited their faithfulness. It was really unbelievable.

That was the end of his life here on earth. We were saddened and grieved, but I found a profound reality to the promise that we do not grieve as those who do not have hope. There was nothing but hope. He finished well.

How is the end of a thing better than its beginning? The reason the end is better is because the end has a future. The end of a thing is where faith becomes sight.

Mr. Austin experienced this.

He is among the most faithful people I have ever known. Not in a flashy, mega platform, quippy sound-bite sort of way that dominates so much of our celebrity culture. Rather, he approached each day with a faithful simplicity, meeting grace in each moment, and in that, his life became a conduit of the grace he received.

Each season, the hard and the beautiful, were woven together . . . redeemed. All the broken things served to make up the beautiful things. And God was glorified. God's glory is the natural outcome of faith. It is the result of living faithfully.

Mr. Austin would often say how deeply grateful he was for God's blessings, and he always wanted God to get the glory. And God did.

In the most miraculous and unexpected way, his past met God's promise. Redemption was his story, and the result was God's glory. He concluded his past. He found hope for his future by being faithful in the moment.

Even this morning as I think about his life and legacy, I recall the everyday ordinary things. Today it is eighty-one degrees outside. He would be dressed in long pants and a sweater, heading out with an expectation that today would be fruitful because all that was necessary was to be faithful.

Soli Deo Gloria. ✳

NOTES

1. Netflix Doesn't Want to Talk About Binge-Watching (investopedia.com).

2. "*Elf* Trivia," IMDb, accessed September 25, 2021, https://www.imdb.com/title/tt0319343/trivia.

3. Rick Warren, "Learn What to Do When You're Pressured to Conform," YouTube, accessed September 25, 2021, https://www.youtube.com/watch?v=F4HlO2a3s7w.

4. Alan Fadling, "Ruthless Elimination of Hurry," Hurried Living, December 18, 2019, accessed September 25, 2021, https://www.unhurriedliving.com/blog/ruthless -elimination-of-hurry.

5. Fadling, "Ruthless Elimination of Hurry."

6. https://www.desiringgod.org/interviews/what-do-you-mean-by-future-grace

7. This story is told in many places. I read about it in Andrew Peterson's book, *Adorning the Dark: Thoughts on Community, Calling, and the Mystery of Making* (Nashville: B&H, 2019).

8. Mike Ashcraft and Rachel Olsen, *My One Word* (Grand Rapids: Zondervan, 2012).